ב"ה

Knowing that God Exists:

The Rational and Evidentiary Support for the Existence of God

Moshe Ben Avraham

2nd Edition

Moshe Ben Avraham

To my parents, who have instructed me in the ways of my ancestors and have always encouraged me to learn as much as I possibly could.

Contents

Acknowledgements

While this text is not particularly long, it represents the culmination of years in the making. I could not have completed this work without the help of others, whom I thank greatly. I would like to thank my parents, who have supported me intellectually, emotionally, and financially, and who have always been there for me in my times of need. I would also like to thank C'zar Bernstein, who introduced me to the majority of the arguments in the book over a period of the last seven or so years. I would also like to thank my Rabbis, who have guided me and helped me grow in my faith: Rabbi David Lehrfield, Rabbi Berl Goldman, And Rabbi Aharon Chaim Notik. This work would have not been possible had it been for all of the support I received, and I am greatly thankful for that.

Introduction

In this book, I will address the most fundamental question underlying the miracle of human life: Whether G-d, as he is traditionally understood in the West, exists. The world has taken a sharply atheistic turn in the last century or so, and I believe that theists, those that believe in G-d, are the proper focus of blame. With modern science, anyone with a cursory understanding of the processes of nature can be an atheist, and feel quite secure that they have everything figured out. With this work, I intend on showing that such confidence is misplaced. G-d is not merely the last resort for those fearing death, nor is he a relic from a more primeval past. Rather, G-d is the best explanation for the fundamental questions of life. I am well aware that G-d cannot be concretely proven or disproven; as such, that is not my goal. My goal will be to show that there is good reason to believe G-d exists, and in fact better reason to believe so than to think he does not. The framework through which you should evaluate the arguments of this paper is quite simple: Given all the evidence provided, is it more likely that G-d exists or that G-d does not exist. I will leave it up to you to make that determination, but I think you will find the evidence for G-d is quite overwhelming. Sections I, II, and III address various arguments in favor of G-d's existence. This is provided through significant evidence and rational exposition. The fourth section provides some common arguments presented by atheists, and refutes them using evidence, reasoning, and/or logical facts. As a whole, I would ask you to approach this work with an open mind, and always attempt to follow the conclusions where the evidence leads. This is a topic that it is extremely easy to become passionate about, but do not feel personally attacked or on edge due to anything in this text. My goal is humble and simple: I seek to teach as many people as I can the truth that I now see. I sincerely hope you enjoy this book, and that you learn from it.

Section I: The Existence of the Universe Necessitates G-d.

Part A: Something Exists

We take for granted the fact that there is existence, and this is acceptable because we only know that things exist because we assume we exist. Our every-day lives happen, and there are objects, people, and other forms of life throughout it all. But lets take a step back from this. Why does anything rather than nothing, exist? I don't mean nothing as in "empty space", but rather even the lack space itself. Nothing, as in literal nonexistence. Nothing, as in what you see from your elbow. Certainly, nothing should exist, as that is the default; but rather than nothing, we have everything we know and experience. It seems to be the case that if nothing existed, nothing should have continued to exist, and I wouldn't be able to be writing this, nor you reading it. Science tells us that everything started with the big bang: a singularity of unimaginable temperature and density expanded outwards at breakneck speed, forming everything that we now experience. But that "solution" to the existence question simply moves the goal; why did that singularity exist rather than not exist? The only reasonable answer is that something <u>outside</u> our universe created it; it could not be inside the universe, because then it would have to create itself. Thomas Aquinas formulated the need for an external cause, in writing that:

The second way is from the nature of the efficient cause. In the world of sense we find there is an order of efficient causes. There is no case known (neither is it, indeed, possible) in which a thing is found to be the efficient cause of itself; for so it would be prior to itself, which is impossible. Now in efficient causes it is not possible to go on to infinity, because in all efficient causes following in order, the first is the cause of the intermediate cause, and the intermediate is the cause of the ultimate cause, whether the intermediate cause be several, or only one. Now to take away the cause is to take away the effect. Therefore, if there be no first cause among efficient causes, there will be no ultimate, nor any intermediate cause. But if in efficient causes it is possible to go on to infinity, there will be no first efficient cause, neither will there be an ultimate effect, nor any intermediate efficient causes; all of which is plainly false. Therefore it is necessary to admit a first efficient cause, to which everyone gives the name of God.[1]

Clearly, as a necessary result of a need for a first cause, G-d must exist. This is because all naturalistic explanations assume the possibility of an infinite causal chain. If we accept that the Big Bang happened, then it was caused by A. But A was caused by B, and B was caused by C. This will continue ad infinitum; science has no desire for determining the first cause, but rather only wants to move the goal so that they can continue to deny G-d. The simple fact is that the Universe needs a cause, and the Big Bang does not fulfill that need. The Kalam Cosmological Argument expresses the truth that the Universe needs a cause, stating thus:

1. Everything that begins to exist has a cause.

2. The universe began to exist.

Therefore,

3. The universe has a cause.

Because this cause cannot be within the universe that exists now, which would lead to self-
contradiction, only something outside space and time could be the origin. Accordingly, what we understand
to be G-d, a timeless, infinite being existing outside the universe, fits the bill perfectly. Non-theists tend to answer this argument with the idea that the Big Bang was the cause. This merely moves the goalpost. If the Big Bang was an explosive expansion of everything, from an unimaginably dense and hot point, wherefrom did this point originate? It is still required to be created,

as it could not have been eternal (The point would never have stayed condensed if the timeframe was forever). As such, the Universe began to exist, and thus needs a creator: G-d.

Part B: Fine-Tuning

The Universe is tailor-made to support intelligent life. This can be seen quite readily in looking at the fundamental constants that make up the "rules" by which the universe operates. These include the charge of an electron, the gravitational constant, and the strength of the nuclear forces, to name a few. If they were to vary by even an unperceivable amount, no life would be possible. In regards to this, Dr. Dennis Scania, the distinguished head of Cambridge University Observatories explains:

If you change a little bit the laws of nature, or you change a little bit the constants of nature--like the charge on the electron--then the way the universe develops is so changed, it is very likely that intelligent life would not have been able to develop.[2]

Professor Robin Collins furthers:

"Over the past thirty years or so, scientists have discovered that just

about everything about the basic structure of the universe is balanced on a razor's edge for life to exist. The coincidences are far too fantastic to attribute this to mere chance or to claim that it needs no explanation. The dials are set too precisely to have been a random accident. Somebody, as Fred Hoyle quipped, has been monkeying with the physics."[3]

I will highlight seven examples of the profound fine-tuning we see throughout the natural world:

First, Entropy and Usable Energy

The natural state of things is disorder; The Second Law of Thermodynamics dictates that total entropy, or disorder, does not decrease. It is surprising then to find that the universe has enough order to allow stars, planets, and life, to prosper. Mathematics Professor Roger Penrose of Oxford University elaborates that the likelihood of the universe having low enough entropy for life is dismally small. He states it takes fine tuning to the degree of:

An accuracy of one part out of ten to the power of ten to the power of 123. This is an extraordinary figure...Even if we were to write a zero on each separate proton and on each separate neutron in the entire universe--and we could throw in all the other particles as well for good measure--we should fall far short of writing down the figure needed.[4]

Second, The Ratio of Constants

The ratio of the gravitational force constant to the electromagnetic force constant...cannot differ from its value by any more than one part in 10^{40} *(one part in ten thousand trillion trillion trillion) without eliminating the possibility for life.* [5]

Third, Gravity

One of the most striking discoveries of modern science has been that the laws and constants of physics unexpectedly conspire in an extraordinary way to make the universe habitable for life. For instance, gravity is fine-tuned to one part in a hundred million billion billion billion billion billion. Chance cannot reasonably account for this "anthropic principle" and that the most-discussed alternative--that there are multiple universes--lacks any evidential support and ultimately collapses upon the realization that these other worlds would owe their existence to a highly designed process.[6]

Fourth, The Cosmological Constant

Lee Strobel discusses the Constant, in his exposition of his interview of aforementioned Professor Robin Collins:

Nobel-winning physicist Steven Weinberg, an avowed atheist, has expressed amazement at the way the cosmological constant--the energy density of empty space--is "remarkably well adjusted in our favor." The constant, which is part of Einstein's equation for General Relativity, could have had any value, positive or negative, "but from first principles one would guess that this constant should be very large," Weinberg said. Fortunately, he added, it isn't: If large and positive, the cosmological constant would act as a repulsive force that increases with distance, a force that would prevent matter from clumping together in the early universe, the process that was the first step in forming galaxies and stars and planets and people. If large and negative, the cosmological constant would act as an attractive force increasing with distance, a force that would almost immediately reverse the expansion of the universe and cause it to recollapse. Either way, life loses--big time. But astonishingly, that's not what has happened. "In fact," Weinberg said, "astronomical observations show that the cosmological constant is quite small, very much smaller than would have been guessed from first principles."

When I asked Collins about this, he told me that the unexpected, counterintuitive, and stunningly precise setting of the cosmological constant "is widely regarded as the single greatest problem facing physics and cosmology today." "How precise is it?" I asked. Collins rolled his eyes. "Well, there's no way we can really comprehend it," he said. "The fine-tuning has conservatively been estimated to be at least one part in a hundred million billion billion billion billion billion. That would be a ten followed by fifty-three zeroes. That's inconceivably precise." He was right--I couldn't imagine a figure like that. "Can you give me an illustration?" I asked. "Put it this way," he said. "Let's say you were way out in space and were going to throw a dart at random toward the Earth. It would be like successfully hitting a bull's eye that's one trillionth of a trillionth of an inch in diameter. That's less than the size of one solitary atom."[7]

Fifth, The Weak Nuclear Force

The nuclear weak force is 10^{28} times the strength of gravity. Had the weak force been slightly weaker, all the hydrogen in the universe would have been turned to helium (making water impossible, for example).[8]

Sixth, The energy of the Big Bang

If the initial explosion of the big bang had differed in strength by as little as 1 part in 10^{60}, the universe would have either quickly collapsed back on itself, or expanded too rapidly for stars to form. In either case, life would be impossible.[9] *As John Jefferson Davis points out an accuracy of one part in 10^{60} can be compared to firing a bullet at a one-inch target on the other side of the observable universe, twenty billion light years away, and hitting the target.*[10]

Seventh, The Proton/Neutron Mass Ratio

If the neutron were not about 1.001 times the mass of the proton, all protons would have decayed into neutrons or all neutrons would have decayed into protons, and thus life would not be possible.[11]

In addition to these seven examples of fundamentals of nature that could not be different without disallowing life, Professor Collins lists five laws of nature that could not be significantly different without providing for a purely abiotic universe. He writes:

The laws and principles of nature themselves have just the right form to allow for the existence embodied moral agents. To illustrate this, we shall consider the following five laws or principles (or causal powers) and show that if any one of them did not exist, self-reproducing, highly complex material systems could not exist: (1) a universal attractive force, such as gravity; (2) a force relevantly similar to that of the strong nuclear force, which binds protons and neutrons together in the nucleus; (3) a force relevantly similar to that of the electro-magnetic force; (4) Bohr's Quantization Rule or something similar; (5) the Pauli Exclusion Principle. If any one of these laws or principles did not exist (and were not replaced by a law or principle that served the same or similar role), complex self-reproducing material systems could not evolve.

First, consider gravity. Gravity is a long-range attractive force between all material objects, whose strength increases in proportion to the masses of the objects and falls off with the inverse square of the distance between them. In classical physics, the amount of force is given by Newton's law. Now consider what would happen if there were no universal, long-range attractive force between material objects, but all the other fundamental laws remained (as much as possible) the same. If no such force existed, then there would be no stars, since the force of gravity is what holds the matter in stars together against the outward forces caused by the high internal temperatures inside the stars. This means that there would be no long-term energy sources to sustain the evolution (or even existence) of highly complex life. Moreover, there probably would be no planets, since there would be nothing to bring material particles together, and even if there were planets (say because planet-sized objects always existed in the universe and were held together by cohesion), any beings of significant size could not move around without floating off the planet with no way of returning. This means that embodied moral agents could not evolve, since the development of the brain of such beings would require significant mobility. For all these reasons, a universal attractive force such as gravity is required for embodied moral agents.

Second, consider the strong nuclear force. The strong nuclear force is the force that binds nucleons (i.e. protons and neutrons) together in the nucleus of an atom. Without it, the nucleons would not stay together. It is actually a result of a deeper force, the "gluonic force," between the quark constituents of the neutrons and protons, a force described by the theory of quantum chromodynamics. It must be strong enough to overcome the repulsive electromagnetic force between the protons and the quantum zero-point energy of the nucleons. Because of this, it must be considerably stronger than the electromagnetic force; otherwise the nucleus would come apart. Further, to keep atoms of limited size, it must be very short range – which means its strength must fall off much, much more rapidly than the inverse square law characteristic of the electromagnetic force and gravity. Since it is a purely attractive force (except at extraordinarily small distances), if it fell off by an inverse square law like gravity or electromagnetism, it would act just like gravity and pull all the protons and neutrons in the entire universe together. In fact, given its current strength, around 10^{40} *stronger than the force of gravity between the nucleons in a nucleus, the universe would most likely consist of a giant black hole.*

Thus, to have atoms with an atomic number greater than that of hydrogen, there must be a force that plays the same role as the strong nuclear force – that is, one that is much stronger than the electromagnetic force but only acts over a very short range. It should be clear that embodied moral agents could not be formed from mere hydrogen, contrary to what one might see on science fiction shows such as Star Trek. One cannot obtain enough self-reproducing, stable complexity. Furthermore, in a universe in which no other atoms but hydrogen could exist, stars could not be powered by nuclear fusion, but only by gravitational collapse, thereby drastically decreasing the time for, and hence probability of, the evolution of embodied moral agents.

Third, consider electromagnetism. Without electromagnetism, there would be no atoms, since there would be nothing to hold the electrons in orbit. Further, there would be no means of transmission of energy from stars for the existence of life on planets. It is doubtful whether enough stable complexity could arise in such a universe for even the simplest forms of life to exist.

Fourth, consider Bohr's rule of quantization, first proposed in 1913, which requires that electrons occupy only fixed orbitals (energy levels) in atoms. It was only with the development of quantum mechanics in the 1920s and 1930s that Bohr's proposal was given an adequate theoretical foundation. If we view the atom from the perspective of classical Newtonian mechanics, an electron should be able to go in any orbit around the nucleus. The reason is the same as why planets in the solar system can be any distance from the Sun – for example, the Earth could have been 150 million miles from the Sun instead of its present 93 million miles. Now the laws of electromagnetism – that is, Maxwell's equations – require that any charged particle that is accelerating emit radiation. Consequently, because electrons orbiting the nucleus are accelerating – since their direction of motion is changing – they would emit radiation. This emission would in turn cause the electrons to lose energy, causing their orbits to decay so rapidly that atoms could not exist for more than a few moments. This was a major problem confronting Rutherford's model of the atom – in which the atom had a nucleus with electrons around the nucleus – until Niels Bohr proposed his ad hoc rule of quantization in 1913, which required that electrons occupy fixed orbitals. Thus, without the existence of this rule of quantization – or something relevantly similar – atoms could not exist, and hence there would be no life.

Finally, consider the Pauli Exclusion Principle, which dictates that no two fermions (spin-one direction and the spin pointing in the opposite direction. This allows for complex chemistry, since without this principle, all electrons would occupy the lowest atomic orbital. Thus, without this principle, no complex life would be possible.[12]

The conclusion that may be drawn from these examples is quite clear: If the atheist is correct, than we are the product of a most preposterously fortunate act of chance. With the extreme precision involved in the preceding cases, the most logical conclusion is that <u>someone</u> or <u>something</u>, I.e. G-d, precisely tuned the Universe to be hospitable to life. Even avowed non-theist Stephen Hawking makes concessions in his book "The Grand Design". He states: "The discovery recently of the extreme fine-tuning of so many laws of nature could lead some to the idea that this grand design has a Grand Designer...True, the laws of the universe seem tailor made for humans."

Section II: The Existence of Life and Humanity Necessitates G-d

Part A: Probability of Abiogenesis

Widely accepted among scientific circles, and rapidly growing in popularity among the common man, is the idea that life arose from non-living matter, and through the guidance provided by natural selection and random mutation has evolved into all the life we see today. The non-theist often believes that materialist and natural processes forming life are de facto law, but in reality there are basic yet fundamental flaws in the line of thought. The fact of the matter is that the probability of life arising from non-life, and then evolving, is so minute that it should scantly be considered as remotely possible. As I will demonstrate, life arising from non-life is simply too improbable a circumstance to be seriously held as belief. You may be wondering why scientists are staunchly in-favor of this evolutionary explanation; quite simply, without the fabricated idea that life arose from the non-living the scientist is hard- pressed to eliminate

G-d from the equation, as was the goal from the beginning.

Before getting into the substance of the discussion, it is important to determine precisely what makes something possible. Simply, something is possible if there are sufficient interactions between particles for something to occur. Professor William Dembski, in his book "The Design Inference", explains precisely how to determine whether something is physically possible, based on the probability of it occurring. He explains that taking into consideration the three relevant factors, there has simply not been enough time since the Big Bang for life to form abiotically. Multiplying the number of elementary particles (which are the indivisible constituent particles of all matter) in the Universe, 10^{80}, The total number of physically possible alterations of the state of matter (based on the Plank Time, the shortest time period possible) per second, 10^{45}, and the total number of seconds the Universe will experience between the Big Bang and the end of the Universe through Heat Death, 10^{25}, yields a product of 10^{150}. This number represents the total number of possible changes all of the particles in the Universe can ever undergo. Accordingly, anything with a probability of less than 1 in 10^{150} cannot physically occur because there are not enough particle interactions to enable such an occurrence.[13]

It is important to understand what this number means. There are 10^{150} possible interactions between particles in the Universe, for all time, from the beginning until the end. As such, if something is less probable then 1 in 10^{150}, it can be considered impossible, because there are simply not enough interactions for that something to occur. With that being said, lets examine some of the probabilities of life forming from non-life:

Professor David Plaisted of

the University of North Carolina writes:

Biologists currently estimate that the smallest life form as we know it would have needed about 256 genes. A gene is typically 1000 or more base pairs long, and there is some space in between, so 256 genes would amount to about 300,000 bases of DNA. The deoxyribose in the DNA ``backbone'' determines the direction in which it will spiral. Since organic molecules can be generated in both forms, the chance of obtaining all one form or another in 300,000 bases is one in two to the 300,000 power. This is about one in 10 to the 90,000 power. It seems to be necessary for life that all of these bases spiral in the same direction. Now, if we imagine many, many DNA molecules being formed in the early history of the earth, we might

have say 10^{100} *molecules altogether (which is really much too high). But even this would make the probability of getting one DNA molecule right about one in 10 to the 89,900 power, still essentially zero. And we are not even considering what proteins the DNA generates, or how the rest of the cell structure would get put together! So the real probability would be fantastically small.*[14]

James F. Coppedge writing for Probability Research in Molecular Biology has remarkably similar findings:

[Even] postulating a primordial sea with every single component necessary for life, speeding up the bonding rate so as to form different chemical combinations a trillion times more rapidly than hypothesized to have occurred, allowing for a 4.6 billion- year-old earth and using all atoms on the earth still leaves the probability of 1 in $10^{119,879}$ *to obtain the minimum set of the required estimate of 239 protein molecules for the smallest theoretical life form. It would require* $10^{119,831}$ *years on the average to obtain a set of these proteins by naturalistic evolution. The number he obtained is* $10^{119,831}$ *greater than the current estimate for the age of the earth (4.6 billion years). In other words, this event is outside the range of probability.*[15]

The basic truth is that the probability of life forming from non-life is so low that it can be considered to be zero. Lets suppose for a second, though, that life did form from non-life and then evolved all of the parts life has today. Nobel Prize winner and discoverer of DNA Professor Francis Crick explains the difficulties faced even in this scenario:

The trouble is that there are about two thousand enzymes, and the chance of obtaining them all in a random trial is only one part in $10^{40,000}$*, an outrageously small probability that could not be faced even if the whole universe consisted of organic soup.*[16]

This truly is the nail in the coffin for evolutionary abiogenesis and its processes; if the entire universe was filled with the proper chemicals in the correct concentrations and ratios, there would still not be even a single cell that came into being. This is simply because the complexity of life is beyond what random chance can produce. Two time Nobel Prize in Chemistry recipient Ilya Prigogine sums it up nicely:

> *The statistical probability that organic structures and the most precisely harmonized reactions that typify living organisms would be generated by accident, is zero.*[17]

The fact of the matter is that every one of these examples exceeds the limit of possibility in this Universe, 10^{150}. Even if only one of them were to be true (and there is strong evidence that they all are), it conclusively proves that life cannot arise from non-life in this Universe. Remember, it isn't even a close call. It is in fact so much more likely that life did not form by chance than the probability than did form by chance that abiogenesis can be entirely thrown out the window. While the scientific community tends to support evolutionary abiogenesis as the reason for the origin of life, this is primarily due to a desire to remove even the possibility for G-d's existence from the equation. There is a greater concern with removing G-d from the discussion than there is with determine what the mathematical and biological truth is. Why is this? Scientists have built their careers on the presupposition that life formed from chemicals, and simply won't admit they were wrong. A similar scenario occurred when evidence for the Big Bang started flowing in; Scientists fought tooth and nail, claiming the Universe to be eternal. Now, we know that is not the case, and the informed also know now that life cannot arise from non-life. It is telling that modern scientists, with all of the knowledge and experience they have, are completely unable to create life from non-life. Intelligent sapient beings are unable to make life; how much more unlikely that life formed by chance. Perhaps even more interesting is the fact that scientists have literally no concept of how life began. Simply put, there are no supported theories that explains life's origin. Professor Klaus

Dose, a leading expert in origin of life studies, lamented in the Journal of Interdisciplinary Science Reviews:

More than 30 years of experimentation on the origin of life in the fields of chemical and molecular evolution have led to a better perception of the immensity of the problem of the origin of life on Earth rather than to its solution. At present all discussions on principal theories and experiments in the field either end in stalemate or in a confession of ignorance. [18]

Part B: Life's Design and Evolution

One of the greatest arguments for G-d's existence is so obvious that people sometimes forget even to mention it. There are those, of course, that do utilize the argument, but I find that it falls to the side in the face of other arguments far too often. The argument I am referring to is that of life. Life is extraordinarily complex, more so than one can reasonably learn in a lifetime, but unraveling just a small piece of its mysteries can enable one to see that G-d must exist. Evolution does not provide a realistic explanation of life's existence. In this section, I will address four areas: The inherent complexity of a cell, DNA, Human feedback loops, and the flagellum. Each of these areas serve as independent supports for the existence of a creator; none can be sufficiently explained by natural selection, and all point to a guided design. Prior to getting into the crux of the arguments, it is important to define a term of art that will be used. "Irreducible

Complexity" refers to the concept that taking away a part of a machine (or a cell, or a biological actor) causes it to no longer function. An example of this would be, as commonly used as an example, a mousetrap; if you remove the spring, for instance, the mousetrap ceases functioning. As you will see, many biological systems are irreducibly complex, and accordingly could not have evolved. For clarity's sake, evolution would not be able to occur because the system would be unable to function without all of its current parts. Evolution depends on gradual change, in small steps, and as such everything that is claimed to be a product of evolution, must be able to be formed from constituent parts, tiny steps at a time. As Charles Darwin stated in "On the Origin of Species", the founding book of the Theory of Evolution,

"If it could be demonstrated that any complex organ existed which could not possibly have been formed by numerous, successive,

slight modifications, my theory would absolutely break down."[19]

In the following pages, I intend to do just that; I will show that various occurrences in the natural world, which have been numerated above, cannot have formed as a result of small, gradual steps. Also important to note is that burden of proof is constantly shifting for the atheist. Whenever presented with an irreducibly complex system, they will literally fabricate a theoretical way in which the system could have evolved, without any real regard to evidence or likelihood. As such, it is not sufficient for the atheist to just provide a means through which a system could evolve, but they must also provide substantive evidence that this occurred. Nevertheless, many systems are simply impossible to have been formed by natural selection, and this fact will soon be elucidated.

To begin, we will look at the immense complexity of a cell. It is best to think of a cell as an unfathomably complicated machine, expertly producing thousand of chemicals needed for life to exist. As Bruce Alberts, President of the National Academy of Sciences writes:

We have always underestimated the cell. . . . The entire cell can be viewed as a factory that contains an elaborate network of interlocking assembly lines, each of which is composed of a set of large protein machines. . . . Why do we call [them] machines? Precisely because, like machines invented by humans to deal efficiently with the macroscopic world, these protein assemblies contain highly coordinated moving parts.[20]

With that being said, a highly important thing to understand is that if you remove just one or two of the thousands and thousands of parts of the cell, it ceases in function. This leads to strong arguments against the supposed evolution of the cell, as it cannot evolve through natural selection if it is not functioning. This is why Biologist and Philosopher Michael Katz argues that cells are too complex to have been formed from small changes:

"In the natural world, there are many pattern-assembly systems for which there is no simple explanation. There are useful scientific explanations for these complex systems, but the final patterns that they produce are so heterogeneous that they cannot effectively be reduced to smaller or less intricate predecessor components. These patterns are, in a fundamental sense, irreducibly complex...Cells and organisms are quite complex by all pattern criteria. They are built of heterogeneous elements arranged in heterogeneous configurations, and they do not self-assemble. One cannot stir together the parts of a cell or of an organism and spontaneously assemble a neuron or a walrus: to create a cell or an organisms one needs a preexisting cell or a preexisting organism, with its attendant complex templates. A fundamental characteristic of the biological realm is that organisms are complex patterns, and, for its

creation, life requires extensive, and essentially maximal, templates."[21]

Looking to specifics, we can see that protein folding is a problem for the evolutionist, as it leads to circular logic. Before we address the details, some background is in order. Proteins are complicated chains of amino-acids, folded in a specific three-dimensional shape that enables them to perform their various biological functions (from chemical signaling to forming muscle tissue, for example). If the protein is not perfectly folded correctly, it will oftentimes not function at all, and can be very detrimental. In the context of irreducible complexity, protein folding becomes a shining example for the need for design. It just so happens that most proteins cannot be formed by cells unless proteins are already present. This of course leads to a case of circular logic: you need proteins to make proteins. In fact, the proteins that help to make other proteins, themselves require other copies of themselves to be present in order to fold properly. Dr. Fazal Rana provides the details of this process:

Many proteins need the assistance of other proteins to fold into the proper three-dimensional shape after they've been produced at the ribosome. The physicochemical properties of amino acid sequences determine the way that the polypeptide chain folds into its complex three-dimensional shape. In a few cases, polypeptide chains will fold into the proper three-dimensional structure on their own. But, most proteins can't, or if they can, the process is slow and inefficient. In the cell's environment, improperly folded proteins or proteins that fold slowly and inefficiently represent a potential catastrophe. In the crowded cell, improperly folded proteins tend to aggregate and form massive clumps that gunk up the cell's operations. To sidestep this potential disaster, virtually every cell throughout the biological realm, from bacteria to humans, relies on a family of proteins called chaperones to encourage efficient and accurate protein folding. Two types of chaperones exist in most organisms: molecular chaperones and chaperonins. Each category consists of numerous proteins that work cooperatively to assist folding. Recent work indicates that parts of the ribosome have chaperone activity helping the newly formed polypeptide chain begin folding. Once released from the ribosome, some proteins adopt their native three-dimensional structure. Others need more help. Several different chaperones will bind to these polypeptides. They help stabilize the partially folded protein, preventing it from aggregating with other proteins in the cell. When these chaperones debind from the polypeptide chain, it folds into its intended three-dimensional shape. Other proteins need more help to fold than chaperones can provide. Once the chaperones disassociate from the partially folded polypeptide chain, these proteins are ushered to chaperonins. These large complexes consist of several polypeptide subunits. Perhaps the best understood chaperonin is GroEL-GroES, found in the bacterium Escherichia coli. The GroEL component of the E. coli chaperonin consists of fourteen subunits that organize into two ringlike structures that stack on top of one another. The stacked rings form a barrellike ensemble with a large open cavity. A partially folded polypeptide is ushered into the GroEL cavity. Another protein complex, GroES, serves as a cap that covers the GroEL cavity. This cavity provides the optimal environment for protein folding. Once properly folded, the polypeptide chain is released from the GroEL cavity after the GroES lid disassociates from the barrel. This overview of protein folding highlights the fact that many proteins cannot fold without proteins. Even chaperones and chaperonins require ribosomes, chaperones, and chaperonins to fold.[22]

The next major area to evaluate is DNA. Deoxyribonucleic Acid, or DNA as we all know it, is the coded instruction set in every cell that guides the process of creating proteins and thus, the rest of both the cell and the body. There are a large number of problems for the evolutionist regarding DNA. The first problem is elucidated by the previously mentioned Dr. Fazal Rana, who explains that proteins and DNA need each other to exist; one cannot be made without the other. He writes:

Biochemists commonly refer to DNA as a self-replicating molecule because its structural properties make it possible to generate two identical daughter molecules from the original parent. In reality, however, DNA cannot replicate on its own...DNA replication requires a myriad of proteins. The synthesis of proteins and the replication of DNA are mutually interdependent. Proteins cannot be produced without DNA, and DNA cannot be produced without proteins-- both hands draw each other.[23]

This paradox, of needing DNA to make protein and protein to make DNA is widely known in science, and has no realistic explanation. As Dr. Rana further elaborates, scientists have come up with a complicated and unsupported theory to eliminate this paradox, but it lacks in both evidence and likelihood.

Dr Rana writes:

Mutual interdependence of DNA and proteins stands as a major stumbling block for evolutionary explanations of life's origin. Origins-of-life researchers even refer to this conundrum as the chicken-and-egg paradox. Because these two molecules are so complex, scientists don't think DNA and proteins could simultaneously arise from a primordial soup. The existence of DNA apart from proteins and proteins apart from DNA is like a column of people trying to simultaneously ascend and descend a staircase. The RNA-world hypothesis has been proposed as a resolution to this paradox. This model maintains that RNA preceded DNA and proteins. RNA can simultaneously store information (like DNA) and catalyze chemical reactions (like proteins). So, it's thought that the RNA world eventually evolved into the DNA-protein world of contemporary biochemistry, with RNA currently functioning as an intermediary between DNA and proteins. While the RNA-world hypothesis rescues the origin-of-life paradigm from the chicken-and-egg paradox on paper, in practical terms it appears largely untenable. Numerous problems abound for the RNA-world hypothesis. For example, it's unlikely that the prebiotic chemical reactions identified in the laboratory for the production of ribose and the nucleobases could take place on early Earth. And, even if these compounds did form, it's unlikely they could assemble into functional RNA molecules. In fact, Leslie Orgel, one of the world's leading origin-of-life researchers, has said, "It would be a miracle if a strand of RNA ever appeared on the primitive Earth." [24]

In addition to the fundamental problems of trying to form DNA without proteins already existing, the second dilemma for the evolutionist is the optimality of DNA's code. DNA is exceptionally efficient at coding for proteins without error; in fact, it is close to the theoretical maximum efficiency in a genetic code. This is great news for us, considering we rely on DNA to make our proteins so that we can survive. This is dreadful news for the evolutionist or the atheist, though, because such an optimal code could not have reasonably been produced by natural selection. Biophysicist Hubert Yockey did the math on the optimality of the genetic code in DNA, to determine how many different codes would have to be tried before finding the optimal current code:

He determined that natural selection would have to explore 1.40 x 10^{70} *different genetic codes to discover the universal genetic code found in nature. The maximum time available for it to originate was estimated at 6.3 x* 10^{15} *seconds. Natural selection would have to evaluate roughly* 10^{55} *codes per second to find the one that's universal. Put simply, natural selection lacks the time necessary to find the universal genetic code.*[25]

As could be expected, there is simply not enough time or available trials for genetic codes to be optimized by natural selection. Keeping in mind that a change in coding wouldn't happen often at all, it is no surprise that the conclusion is against evolution. We can look to Paleobiologists Douglas Erwin and James Valentine, who explain why evolution is too rare to realistically be a source of change:

"Viable mutations with major...effects are exceedingly rare and usually infertile; the chance of two identical rare mutant individuals arising in sufficient propinquity to produce offspring seems too small to consider as a significant evolutionary event. These problems of viable "hopeful monsters" ... render these explanations untenable"[26]

The next problem with DNA being evolved through natural selection is that Bacteria and Eukaryotes (which form most living organisms, such as plants and animals) do not share the same enzymes used in the replication of DNA, but do share its optimal coding mechanism and other traits. This means that two near identical systems of coding would have to have evolved independently twice, and still result in virtually the same system, less some enzymes. Given that natural selection and evolution are entirely random, it is essentially impossible for this to occur. Random chance doesn't produce consistent results across trials, and that is precisely what we see in this case. The conclusion of the researchers that discovered this stunning breakthrough, Leipe et al, is thus:

Surprisingly, in 1999 researchers from the National Institutes of Health demonstrated that the core enzymes in the DNA replication machinery of bacteria and archaea/ eukaryotes (the two major trunks of the evolutionary tree of life) did not share a common evolutionary origin. From an evolutionary perspective, it appears as if two identical DNA replication systems emerged independently in bacteria and archaea-- after these two evolutionary lineages supposedly diverged from the last universal common ancestor. (If evolutionary processes explain the origin of DNA replication, then two different systems should exist in archaea and bacteria.)[27]

This discovery alone drives a nail in the coffin of evolution. It is virtually impossible (if not entirely impossible) for two unrelated organisms to form the same system of coding; that simply is not how chance works. It is akin to you and your best friend flipping ten-thousand coins each, and both you having the exact same result, coin for coin. Except in this instance, it is far, far more coins then that.

The last area we will evaluate as to why DNA is evidence for an intelligent designer is that the very fact that DNA contains coded information is evidence of G-d. Evolution by nature cannot add information to a genetic code; it only mutates it. But this code had to originate somewhere, and without a functional genetic code no replication, and thus no evolution, could occur. Journalist and researcher Lee Strobel explains that the information inherent in DNA cannot by definition form from random action, in his interview with Professor Stephen Meyer:

The six-feet of DNA coiled inside every one of our body's one hundred trillion cells contains a four-letter chemical alphabet that spells out precise assembly instructions for all the proteins from which our bodies are made. Cambridge-educated Stephen Meyer demonstrated that no hypothesis has come close to explaining how information got into biological matter by naturalistic means. On the contrary, he said that whenever we find a sequential arrangement that's complex and corresponds to an independent pattern or function, this kind of information is always the product of intelligence. "Books, computer codes, and DNA all have these two properties," he said. "We know books and computer codes are designed by intelligence, and the presence of this type of information in DNA also implies an intelligent source." In addition, Meyer said the Cambrian explosion's dazzling array of new life forms, which suddenly appeared fully formed in the fossil record, with no prior transitions, would have required the infusion of massive amounts of new biological information. "Information is the hallmark of mind," said Meyer. "And purely from the evidence of genetics and biology, we can infer the existence of a mind that's far greater than our own--a conscious, purposeful, rational, intelligent designer who's amazingly creative."[28]

Without beating a dead horse, it is safe to say that DNA cannot have abiotic origins. There are simply too many unresolved problems, and too many near-impossible (or simply impossible) events that would need to occur.

With that, we can next address human feedback loops. In humans, homeostasis (or the body's self-regulation) is controlled by hundreds of different feedback loops, which is just a way of saying that there are systems that balance each other by detecting relevant levels of hormones or proteins, to ensure a level that is conducive to life. The problem for evolution here, is that the feedback systems would only be functional, if both the organ(s), gland(s), and sensory mechanisms were all in place. Remove one, and the homeostatic mechanism is destroyed. As such, human feedback loops can be said to be irreducibly complex. As Dr. Geoffrey Simons explains:

The endocrine system includes the pituitary, thyroid, and adrenal glands, the testes and ovaries, and numerous smaller islands of tissue located in the pancreas, heart, lungs, kidneys, stomach, liver, and placenta. Each gland produces specific hormones that carry messages to target cells, telling them what to do, when, and how. To date there are more than 40 hormones known, and the production of each one is controlled by a feedback loop. Many work in parallel or tandem, some compete, and some have double or triple feedback loops. The overall complexity, the necessity for WPP--whole package phenomenon--and the need for all systems to be in place simultaneously strongly challenge[s] evolutionary theory...Hundreds of different feedback loops are at work in the human body, crisscrossing, overlapping, and interacting with each other all day long. They involve millions of compounds that know exactly how to find their target cells. These cells know what to do with each message. A single cell might receive TSH, GH, LH, and FSH [various hormones] multiple times in the same hour. The endocrine processes often interact with each other ... Nearly all these hormones had to have appeared simultaneously, along with their target cells, and the feedback loops. [29]

The Human body cannot exist without maintaining homeostasis, and that is only possible if feedback loops re already in place. This not only applies to humans, though, but rather any organism must maintain homeostasis through feedback loops. As demonstrated by Dr. Simons, these are irreducibly complex, as such and cannot function without being in their completed state. There is no reasonable explanation on how this would function through an evolutionary process, and it is not hard to see how such a system would need to be complete for functioning.

The last area to evaluate as to the design of life and evolution is the bacterial flagellum. This is a protrusion on the outside of a bacteria, much like a tiny tail, that moves like a motor to propel the cell. Both the production and use of the flagellum are irreducibly complex, and either serves as an independent argument for the existence of a creator.

First, we will evaluate the creation of a flagellum. S. Kalir et al, writing for the journal Science explains:

The production of the bacterial flagellum resembles a well-orchestrated manufacturing process. Its assembly pathway displays an exquisite molecular logic that results in the orderly production of this particular motor. Each step in the process seems to have been planned with subsequent steps in mind. The information required to produce the more than forty proteins that make up the bacterial flagellum resides with the bacteria's DNA. In bacteria, genes specifying proteins involved in the same cellular process often lie next to one another along the DNA molecule. Biochemists use the term operon to describe a grouping of these juxtaposed genes. The flagellar genes, organized into over fourteen different operons, cluster into three operon classes: Class 1, Class 2, and Class 3. The flagellar operons are typically "turned off," making no proteins until the bacterial cell "senses" that the time has arrived to produce flagella. When this happens, the Class 1 operons "turn on" directing the production of two proteins. The two Class 1 proteins, in turn, activate Class 2 operon genes. The Class 2 operons turn on one at a time according to the spatial positioning of the proteins within the flagellum. Proteins forming the innermost structures of the flagellum, such as the rotor and stator, are produced first followed by the proteins forming the drive shaft and bushings. Once the stator, rotor, drive shaft, and bushing (called the basal body) have been assembled, the Class 3 operons turn on and the Class 2 operons shut down. The genes of the Class 3 operons produce the proteins that form the universal joint and whiplike flagellum. This well-orchestrated process of gene expression ensures that the proper proteins are present at the proper time during the assembly of the flagellum. The cell avoids wasting precious resources by making proteins only when needed. Additionally, improper assembly of the flagellum will result if proteins are made ahead of time. For example, if the cell makes the protein forming the whiplike flagellum before the basal body comes together, this protein will assemble into a whiplike structure inside the cell. Watching almost any manufacturing process evokes appreciation for the efficient and orderly production that depends on careful planning, design, and engineering. Witnessing the assembly of bacterial flagella elicits the same type of response. The biochemical pathway to their structure and assembly evokes a sense of awe at the engineering brilliance involved. [30]

As you can see through the numerous and precise steps needed to create the flagellum, there is little to no possibility that it was produced by random chance. It is quite obvious that a designer is needed for such a complex process, involving many steps and proper timing; random mutations don't produce orderly designs. The evolutionist would assert "Yes, they do." The problem with that rebuke is that there is no evidence of such. There are no incomplete, non- functioning flagellum in the literature, and even if there was, having half of a tail doesn't provide a survival advantage, and thus would be minimized through evolution. In addition to the creation of a flagellum being irreducibly complex, the function is as well. Biochemistry Professor Michael Behe explains that a swimming system requires three parts: A paddle, a rotor, and a motor. In a human that is swimming, for example, the hand is the paddle, the arm is the rotor, and the muscles of the arms and torso are the motor. Remove any one of these three, and it fails to work. The same can be said for the flagellum, as Professor Behe writes:

The rotary nature of the bacterial flagellar motor was a startling, unexpected discovery. Unlike other systems that generate mechanical motion (muscles, for example) the bacterial motor does not directly use energy that is stored in a "carrier" molecule such as ATP. Rather, to move the flagellum it uses the energy generated by a flow of acid through the bacterial membrane. The requirements for a motor based on such a principle are quite complex and are the focus of active research. A number of models for the motor have been suggested; none of them are simple. The bacterial flagellum uses a paddling mechanism. Therefore it must meet the same requirements as other such swimming systems. Because the bacterial flagellum is necessarily composed of at least three parts-- a paddle, a rotor, and a motor-- it is irreducibly complex. Gradual evolution of the flagellum, therefore faces mammoth hurdles. The general professional literature on the bacterial flagellum is about as rich as the literature on the cilium, with thousands of papers published on the subject over the years. That isn't surprising; the flagellum is a fascinating biophysical system, and flagellated bacteria are medically important. Yet here again, the evolutionary literature is totally missing. Even though we are told that all biology must be seen through the lens of evolution, no scientist has ever published a model to account for the gradual evolution of this extraordinary molecular machine.[31]

Accordingly, it is quite clear that the flagellum is irreducibly complex, for multiple distinct reasons. More than that, though, through all the examples I have provided, we can see that in the world, there exist biological structures that could not have formed by random chance and mutation. This is very strong evidence for G-d. Now, it is true that most scientists do not agree that evolution is false; that hardly matters though. At one point, most "scientists" thought that the world was flat, and that the Earth was the center of the

Universe. An appeal to a majority is not a proper response, nor is derision. The only refutation to these arguments must be specific to the argument itself, and directly addressing the claims made (which are in fact well supported by evidence). I am quite confident that no significant evidence to the contrary can be provided, and any claims otherwise must be approached from a critical and analytical perspective.

Part C: Human Consciousness

Humans are unique in the world, in more ways than one. We are the world's best distance runners, we display extraordinary ability to adapt to our surroundings, and we grow hair on our heads with little elsewhere. More than that though, we are sapient. We feel, we express, we speak. We form complex thoughts and convey ideas, building upon the ideas of others, and we create not only tools but structures, materials, vehicles, and space ships. The real mystery, though, is our sense of self. We are individuals; we have our own wants and needs and desires, and we experience all of life first person. Consider what it means to be a human. We look out through our eyes, and manipulate the world with our dexterous hands and limbs. The real question, though, is our mind. As far as we can tell, no other living organism has a mind, an internal dialogue that allows us to make decisions and weigh costs versus benefits. But a mind is more than that. For all intents and purposes, we are our mind. Everything is computed through our mind, and our individuality is tied explicably to our mind. There is good reason to think that this mind is more than simple chemical reactions in a material brain; that is, our mind is non-material, something other than matter. This position is known as dualism: the proposition that our minds are distinct from our bodies. Below I will present an argument for our minds being distinct from our bodies; if this is the case, it forms strong reason to believe that G-d exists, because it follows from the existence of non-material minds, I.e. Souls.

The Mind and Body are fundamentally different:

Keith Maslin states:

"Physical occurrences do not just appear to be different from consciousness; they are utterly different, so utterly different in fact,

that it is inconceivable how the physical could produce the mental."[32]

William Lane Craig elaborates:

Mental events such as thoughts, feelings of pain and sensory experiences do not contain physical qualities like mass, spatial dimensions and space location, are not composed of chemicals, and do not have electrical properties.[33]

There are two types of things in the world, as far as we can tell through common experience: physical objects, such as a desk or a car, and subjective experiences, like love or the color red. Lets take colors for example. Blue looks a particular way; that is, it appears to us in a consistent manner. Orange has another particular look, that we know looks different than blue. This particular "blueness" or "orangeness" has its own quality, being in that particular color. To use another example, take physical sensations. Pain feels a certain way, and so does hunger. These sensations feel like themselves; they have the quality of feeling a certain way. It "is" something to be human; it is not something to be a robot. Robots do not have the internal dialogue we do, much less the minds needed to even have such. What separates us from robots then? A mind.

This mind is non-physical, as otherwise we could simply give a robot one. But we cannot, and science is no closer to understanding the material basis for the mind than it was 100 years ago. Renowned Philosopher David Hume furthers:

It must be confessed, moreover, that perception, and that which depends on it are inexplicable by mechanical cause, that is by figures and motions. And supposing there were a machine so constructed as to think, feel and have perception, we could conceive of it as enlarged and yet preserving the same proportions, so that we might enter it as a mill. And this granted, we should only find on visiting it, pieces which push one against another, but never anything by which to explain a perception. This must be sought for, therefore, in the simple substance and not in the composite or in the machine.[34]

Simply put, we have minds, and there is no evidence to suggest that it is produced by the brain (The brain can influence the mind, such as when intoxicated, but the brain cannot be shown to produce our minds). Our minds appear in virtually every aspect to be distinct from our bodies, and this has even worked its way into the common lexicon: If I ask, "Do you have a body?", you would most likely reply in the affirmative. What then, is the "you" that has the body? Your mind, separate from what you really are. Distinguished Professor of Philosophy at Biola University J.P. Moreland elaborates on the inability of science to determine the origins of the mind, stating:

The truth is that naturalism has no plausible way to explain the appearance of emergent mental properties in the cosmos. Ned Block confesses that we have no idea how consciousness could have emerged from nonconscious matter: "we have nothing--zilch--worthy of being called a research programme. . . . Researchers are stumped" (Block 1994, p. 211). John Searle says this is a "leading problem in the biological sciences" (Searle 1995, p. 61). Colin McGinn observes that consciousness seems like "a radical novelty in the universe" (McGinn 1999, p. 14); he wonders how our "technicolour" awareness can "arise from soggy grey matter" (McGinn 1991, pp. 10–1). David Papineau wonders why consciousness emerges: "to this question physicalists 'theories of consciousness' seem to provide no answer" (Papineau 1993, p. 119). Papineau's solution is to deny the reality of consciousness as a genuinely mental phenomenon (Papineau 1993, pp. 106, 114–8, 120, 121, 126). He correctly sees that strong physicalism is the only real alternative for a naturalist.[35]

The late Harvard Professor B.F. Skinner continues that:

Evolutionary theorists have suggested that 'conscious intelligence' is an evolved trait, but they have never shown how a nonphysical variation could arise [in the first place] to be selected by physical contingencies of survival. [36]

Based on this, Jaegwon Kim succinctly concludes:

If a whole system of phenomena that are prima facie not among basic physical phenomena resists physical explanation, and especially if we don't even know where or how to begin, it would be time to reexamine one's physicalist commitments. [37]

While so far I have mainly addressed the failings of science in explaining the mind, it is worth noting that there are positive arguments for the mind being non-physical. Professor Edward Feser makes the argument that the mind is non-physical due to its intentionality, that is, its ability to act with purpose; nothing non-living in the universe acts with purpose, only life does. This seems to imply that life has a quality that grants purpose, and this quality cannot be physical, as nothing physical has purpose (unless it is already alive). He writes:

More to the point, brain processes, composed as they are of meaningless chemical components, seem as inherently devoid of intentionality as soundwaves or ink marks. Any intentionality they would also have to be derived from something else. But if anything physical would be devoid of intrinsic intentionality, whatever does have intrinsic intentionality would thereby have to be non-physical. Sine the mind is the source of the intentionality of physical entities like sentences and pictures, and doesn't get its intentionality from anything else (there's no one "using" our minds to convey meaning) it seems to follow that the mind has intrinsic intentionality, and thus is non-physical. [38]

Feser *continues that:*

> *Talk of purposes and functions, if taken literally, seems to presuppose intentionality; in particular it seems to presuppose the agency of an intelligence of one who design something for a particular purpose. But the aim of Darwinian evolutionary theory is to explain biological phenomena in a manner that involves no appeal to intelligent design. . . . Just as modern physics has tended to explain phenomena by carving off the subjective qualitative appearances of things and relocating them into the mind, so to did the Darwinian revolution in biology push purpose and function out of the biological realm, making them out to be mind-dependent and devoid of objective reality.* [39]

It is quite clear that life has the distinguishing characteristic of purpose, which can only be attained from something non-physical (because non-life has no purpose). Therefore we have established a positive argument for life having a non-material mind, as the mind is the originator of purpose.

Part D: Human Reason and Truth

For the atheist, we have all the traits that we currently have either because they aided in survival, or did not hurt survival. That type of explanation works in some cases: Our molars are flat(ish) to grind plant matter, while our canines are sharp(ish) to tear meat. Our pupils constrict in sunlight to enable less obscured vision and protect the retina for harm. It makes sense that traits that are beneficial will be passed on, while those without them are less likely to reproduce. As shown in Part A of this section, though, the mathematical probability of evolution producing current life is slim to none. Nevertheless, the "scientist" clings to the naturalistic explanation, in no small part because he wants job security. That aside, there is something else about humanity that simply cannot be explained by evolution and naturalism: Our capacity for reason and truth. There is no evolutionary reason that our minds be capable of deciphering deep truths and utilizing reasoning; our minds, if the evolutionary story is to be believed, should only do what is best for survival, not universal truth. C.S. Lewis elaborates on this disjunct between survival reactions and the knowledge we possess. He writes:

> *Once, then, our thoughts were not rational. That is, all our thoughts once were, as many of our thoughts still are, merely subjective events, not apprehensions of objective truth. Those which had a cause external to ourselves at all were (like our pains) responses to stimuli. Now natural selection could operate only by eliminating responses that were biologically hurtful and multiplying those which tended to survival. But it is not conceivable that any improvement of responses could ever turn them into acts of insight, or even remotely tend to do so. The relation between response and stimulus is utterly different from that between knowledge and the truth known. Our physical vision is a far more*

useful response to light than that of the cruder organisms which have only a photo-sensitive spot. But neither this improvement nor any possible improvements we can suppose could bring it an inch nearer to being a knowledge of light. It is admittedly something without which we could not have had that knowledge. But the knowledge is achieved by experiments and inferences from them, not by refinement of the response. It is not men with specially good eyes who know about light, but men who have studied the relevant sciences. In the same way our psychological responses to our environment our curiosities, aversions, delights, expectations-could be indefinitely improved (from the biological point of view) without becoming anything more than responses.[40]

It does not take an abundance of thought to see Lewis' point as correct. If the evolutionist is to be believed, our ancestors were microscopic organisms, likely the size of a bacteria, that acted by responding to stimuli, similar in manner to how you pull your hand away instantly from a hot kettle. There is no logical scenario in which these essentially mindless responses develop through the generations into something capable of reason and the acquisition of truth. Even more decisive a blow against evolution and materialism is that if the mind is solely a physical construct, there are self-contradictions that occur. Evolutionary biologist J.B.S. Haldane explains:

""If my mental processes are determined wholly by the motions of atoms in my brain I have no reason to suppose that my beliefs are true. They may be sound chemically, but that does not make them sound logically. And hence I have no reason for supposing my brain to be composed of atoms."[41]

The fact that we are able to decipher the world around us while experiencing the subjective is evidence by itself that there is more to the mind than mere atoms. Non-life can't think, and almost certainly never will. But the real surprise is that we can think. Without substantial hoop-jumping the materialist is unable to explain our ability to acquire truth, and therefore the simplest explanation is a divinely placed mind.

Part E: Near-Death Experiences

A near-death experience or NDE is a phenomenon in which a person that is near death has a vivid mental experience of perceiving the divine. This often includes seeing dead relatives, walking down a bright tunnel, and seeing G-d himself. The experiences are almost always pleasant, and life changing. These experiences occur even when the patient is brain-dead, meaning there is zero brain activity. Furthermore, these experiences are extremely common, as George Gallup Jr. Found:

"15 percent of all Americans who almost died - - whether in accidents, surgeries, drug overdoses or attempted suicides - - reported near-death experiences. Of that number, 9 percent had out-of-body experiences, in which they experienced their souls looking down at their bodies; 11 percent reported entering different realms such as heaven or hell, and 8 percent said they saw spiritual beings. It was found that the likelihood of having a

near-death experience was hardly affected by prior religious belief or knowledge of near-death experiences"[42]

During these experiences, unexplainable events sometimes occur, such as the blind being able to see. Patrick Wells writes:

In one of his books, "Mindsight", Dr. Ken Ring investigated...blind people who had near-death-experiences and or out-of-body experiences. 80% of the respondents claimed that they were able to see when out of their bodies, even those who were congenitally blind (blind from birth). Congenitally blind people don't even have a concept of sight; they only dream in audio. Many of these people had flat brain waves and were in cardiac arrest in hospitals. Five of them saw things that could be verified independently. [43]

This alone serves as a very strong piece of evidence for the existence of the afterlife and therefore of G-d. Those blind from birth have no conception of sight; they can't describe what it is like, having never experienced it for themselves. Following a near-death experience, large numbers of people that are blind, a full 80% of them, are able to say that they saw. Until there is a solid scientific explanation (don't hold your breath, there will never be one), we should default to what the evidence says and agree that G-d exists. Important to note is that there is no real scientific explanation for these events. Dr. Peter Fenwick writes that:

"The brain isn't functioning. It's not there. It's destroyed. It's abnormal. But, yet, it can produce these very clear experiences ... an unconscious state is when the brain ceases to function. For example, if you faint, you fall to the floor, you don't know what's happening and the brain isn't working. The memory systems are particularly sensitive to unconsciousness. So, you won't remember anything. But, yet, after one of these

experiences [a NDE], you come out with clear, lucid memories ... This is a real puzzle for science."[44]

A comprehensive study from the Netherlands found that no medical explanation is sufficient for explaining the phenomenon of NDEs. It states:

> *Medical factors including psychological, neuropsychological or physiological factors cannot account for the occurrence and experience of an NDE. In other words, all the physical explanations for this experience like fear of death, oxygen deprivation, drugs, hallucinations, a dying pineal gland, or the brain helping us die by mitigating our fear with endorphins, etc. cannot adequately explain this phenomenon.*[45]

When all of this evidence is taken in context, it becomes clear that there is something more at play than trickery by the brain. Near death experiences provide a brief glimpse into what lies beyond, and therefore provide solid evidence for the existence of G-d.

Part F: Universal Morality

Morality is something that is held in high regard by many people, and generally speaking we all try to do what we believe is the right thing to do. As I will illustrate, moral objectivity, the idea that there is an absolute right and wrong, has no basis without G-d. It will become clear that without G-d to define morality, there really is no such thing.

The neo-Darwinian school of thought, embraced by atheists and naturalists, holds that life started from non life by random chance, and evolved through natural selection to be over the eons molded into its current form. There are several implications to this idea. The most striking is that we are not truly accountable for our actions. Under neo-Darwinism, we are a product of chemical reactions, and chemical reactions have no moral weight. While many atheists live moral lives (to the extent that is possible without G-d), the morals they adhere to are rooted in common discourse, or what they intuitively feel is right. The problem with this type of morality, is that if it is left to the people to decide, there will be dramatic and obviously immoral events that occur, that society simply looks away from out of fear of ostracism or heartfelt belief that the events are justified. The epitome of the modern example of such an event is the Holocaust. People believed that the state determined morality, and as such perpetrated a genocide of the Jewish People. This type of occurrence is a necessary event whenever the people decide that there is only the morality of man. Another morose example would be the horrors perpetrated by the Soviet Union against their own people, where tens of millions died so that Soviet Figureheads straight out of 1984 could exert their power and attempt to become as powerful as the G-d they denied existed.

Now, the difficult matter at hand is to show that objective morals do exist. I will provide good reason to think it is true. Ultimately, it is incumbent on the reader to decide for themselves: Are some things absolutely good or evil, or is everything only what society decides it is? When we speak in terms of morality, we tend to be speaking of moral duties; those things which we are obligated to do by morality, such as stopping a rape from occurring. The problem for the atheist is that moral duties only make sense if G-d exists. Richard Taylor explains:

A duty is something that is owed . . . . But something can be owed only to some person or persons. There can be no such thing as duty in isolation . . . . The idea of political or legal obligation is clear enough . . . . Similarly, the idea of an obligation higher than this, and referred to as moral obligation, is clear enough, provided reference to some lawmaker higher . . . . than those of the state is understood. In other words, our moral obligations can . . . be understood as those that are imposed by God. This does give a clear sense to the claim that our moral obligations are more binding upon us than our political obligations . . . . But what if this higher-than-human lawgiver is no longer taken into account? Does the concept of a moral obligation . . . still make sense? . . . . the concept of moral obligation [is] unintelligible apart form the idea of God. The words remain, but their meaning is gone.[46]

As you can see, it seems to be the case that morality only makes sense logically in the context of G-d. To delve deeper into this, and attempt to decidedly show the existence of G-d, I present the following argument, the premises of which I will individually support below:

1. Either G-d Exists or He does not Exist

2. If G-d does not exist, objective moral values do not exist.

3. There are evils in existence.

C4. Therefore, objective moral values do exist.

C5. Therefore, G-d Exists.

Premise 1: Either G-d Exists or He does not Exist

Logically, there are only two possibilities; either G-d exists, or G-d does not exist. There is no "middle ground" between the two, where G-d would 'partially' exist, whatever that means. This is summed up in the Law of Excluded Middle, a logical law which states that either "A", or "Not A" is true. It is intuitive if you think about it: Someone cannot be both going to the store, and not going to the store–they logically contradict. The same can be said about everything; either it is, or it is not. In regards to G-d, we can see that it makes perfect sense, and in fact any alternative would fail to make sense, that either G-d exists or He does not exist.

Premise 2: If G-d does not exist, objective moral values do not exist.

I alluded to this premise previously, in discussing the moral backing (or lack thereof) of Neo-Darwinin thought. Nevertheless, I will reiterate and expand upon what has been said. If G-d does not exist, and we are merely the naturalistic product of evolution and natural selection, our "moral compass" is merely a survival tool, and has no basis in determining truth. Accordingly, objective moral values would not exist, because "morals" are just a name we give to chemical reactions in the body that trigger a response. Objective moral values, or moral values that are true independent of other variables, cannot exist without G-d, as without G-d nothing is actually right or wrong. Suppose for a minute that a rebuttal to this point is made, saying "Society defines morality, and thus morals are objective to the society." There are a couple of responses to this argument. The first is that what society defines as moral changes with time and with new members of the society; this means any such morals are not in fact objective, but are instead only rules that some members abide by. Another response is that society could choose to make things that are clearly and intuitively wrong be "morally correct". For example, slavery was deemed to be perfectly fine morally prior to the Civil War in the US, but that doesn't mean it was actually right. Without G-d to define morals, we are left to our own devices, and what is write or wrong changes by the day; this is not objectivity, it is absurdity.

Premise 3: There are evils in existence.

This premise is certainly the most difficult to prove, within the argument that I provided, as it ultimately comes down to individual belief. That being said, if this premise is either found to be true, or held to be true by the reader, there is no possibility to deny the following two conclusions. The first line defense for supporting this premise is that in common experience, we hold morals to be objective. Rape is wrong. Murder is wrong. These are not things that are wrong simply because the government has decreed so; these are injustices that are morally wrong by their very nature. The support for this claim is simply intuitive. If we travelled to a poor country gripped by civil war, and found someone executing children, we would know that it is wrong to do so; not because our government or our parents told us, but because it is something we simply intuitively know. Now the atheistic response to this would be that this intuitive knowledge is simply a product of evolution. The problem with this is that many things we regard as immoral would be advantageous in a naturalistic evolutionary setting. Rape, rather than being horrible, would be an easy way to ensure your genes are passed on. Murder could be considered a viable way to secure resources and mates. Burglary could be simply acquiring resources of the less-capable of defense. As you can see, our moral compass, which dictates all these examples as terrible things to do, is not based on evolutionary advantage, but rather on an independent moral framework–that created by G-d. Going back to the original intention of this premise, it is quite clear that there are things that are morally evil in the world. Serial killers, child abuse, poverty, all of these can be seen as moral evils. To the avowed atheist, this may not be the case (as agreeing necessarily leads to G-d), but to the majority of us, we see evils in the world around us.

Conclusions: Objective Moral Values Exist and therefore G-d Exists

The first conclusion, the Objective Moral Values exist, follows logically from acceptance of the third premise, that evil exists. If evil exists, than it is objectively wrong, and its simple to see how objective morals are a necessity following that. That G-d exists follows logically from the first four premises; if there are no objective moral values without G-d, and there are objective moral values in our experience, then G-d exists.

The important thing to remember in regards to the moral argument for G-d, is that if there is no G-d, there is no reason for anyone to act morally. Society may look down upon transgressors, but if there is no divine judge, no one will truly be held accountable for their misdeeds. As I have shown through the syllogism presented previously, there is strong reason based on morality to believe in the existence of G-d.

Section III: The Existence of the Jewish People and Torah Necessitates G-d.

Part A: National Revelation

The Jewish religion differs from all other religions in regards to how it began. In most (or all) other religions, a man (e.g. Jesus or Muhammad) or a small group of men (The Apostles) initiated a claim that divine actions occurred, and from thenceforth the religion grew. The problem with relying on this type of claim is that it could easily be fabricated, altered, or the supposed events may not have occurred at all. Now the question arises: How can one avoid the preceding types of disputes and uncertainties? The answer is quite simple: more people must bear witness. This is the standard that we apply throughout our lives; if one person says the moon is purple, we aren't likely to believe them, but if the entire population of the State of Florida saw a purple moon, then we would tend to take their word for it. This is not to say that a majority couldn't be wrong, but especially in addressing historical events, more people confirming the story is good reason to believe it. Lets look at the origin of Judaism with this in mind. In the biblical record (which has never been disproven as a source of historical events, and to the contrary has significant support in archeological findings), Moses lead the Hebrews out of Egypt, and they ended up at Mt. Sinai. There, the entire Jewish nation, numbering 3 million or more, heard G-d speak to them. As it is written in the Torah:

"You have been shown in order to know that God, He is the Supreme Being. There is none besides Him. From heaven he let you hear His voice in order to teach you, and on earth He showed you His great fire, and you heard His words amid the fire."[47]

This is quite the claim, that an entire nation experienced divine revelation. In fact, it is the only such claim ever made in recorded history, which the Torah successfully predicts to be the case:

You might inquire about times long past, from the day that God created man on earth, and from one end of heaven to the other: Has there ever been anything like this great thing or has anything like it been heard? Has a people ever heard the voice of God speaking from the midst of the fires as you have heard and survived?[48]

The reason for this is quite simple: it is nearly impossible to fabricate. Lets see why. There are two possibilities: either the Jewish People experienced national divine revelation, or they did not. If they did, there is no argument because we agree. It becomes interesting though, if they did not. If they did not experience national divine revelation, someone at some point had to come up with the story that they did. There are multiple problems with this:

1. There are obvious difficulties in convincing an entire people that either they, or their ancestors, experienced G-d directly. No one would agree to believe strongly enough to teach it to their kids with such fervor that it would continue for

3800 years. Rabbi Moshe Zeldman explains the nonsensical nature of such a hoax:

Perhaps a hoax such as this could have been attempted at a later period in history. Perhaps the claim of national revelation did not originate at Sinai, but began, for example, 1,000 years after the event was said to have occurred. Perhaps the leader Ezra, for example, appears on the scene, introducing a book purported to be written by God and given to a people who stood at Sinai a long time ago.

Could someone get away with this kind of hoax? For example, would you believe the following:

"I want to let you in on a very little-known, but true fact. In 1794 over 200 years ago, from May until August, the entire continent of North America mysteriously sank under the sea. For those four months, the whole continent was submerged and somehow all animal, plant and human life managed to adapt to these bizarre conditions. Then, on August 31, the entire continent suddenly floated up to the surface and life resumed to normal."

Is there a possibility that I'm telling the truth? Do you know for a fact that it is a lie? After all, it happened so long ago, how do you know it didn't happen? Maybe you learned about in school and just forgot about it.

A significant event with many eyewitnesses cannot be perpetuated as a hoax.

You know that North America did not sink hundreds of years ago for one simple reason: If it did, you would have heard about it. An event so unique and amazing, witnessed by multitudes of people would have been known, discussed, and passed down, becoming a part of history. The fact that no one has heard of it up until now means you know the story is not true, making it impossible to accept. An event of great significance with a large number of eyewitnesses cannot be perpetuated as a hoax. If it did not happen, everyone would realize it is false since no one ever heard about it before. Thus, if such an event was indeed accepted as part of history, the only way to understand its acceptance is that the event actually happened.[49]

2. If the claim was that Hebraic ancestors experienced revelation, why do we have no record of anyone bringing this amazing discovery to light? One would think that the discoverer of the "lost" religion would be a very important figure. This is especially telling given the fact that Jews are some of the best historical record keepers in the world; there is simply no chance that while recording every ruling of every Rabbi for thousands of years, no one thought to record even a small indication that someone made up the Sinai Account.

3. The Exodus and Sinai story is universal through the Jewish people; there are no Jews that think there were 11 plagues, or that the red sea froze so the Jews could walk across it. Why are there no outliers? Simply because the story is passed down directly and exactly. Rabbi Nechemia Coopersmith furthers on the historicity of the Sinai revelation:

Let's assume for the moment that the revelation at Mount Sinai is really a hoax; God did not write the Torah. How did the revelation at Sinai become accepted for thousands of years as part of our nation's history?

Imagine someone trying to pull off such a hoax. An Ezra figure shows up one day holding a scroll.

"Hey Ezra – what are you holding there?"

"This is the Torah."

"The Torah? What's that?"

"It's an amazing book filled with laws, history and stories. Here, take a look at it."

Very nice, Ezra. Where did you get this?"

"Open up the book and see what it says. This book was given thousands of years ago to your ancestors. Three million of them stood at Mount Sinai and heard God speak! God appeared to everyone, giving His law and instruction."

How would you respond to such a claim?

The people give Ezra a quizzical look and say,

"Wait a second, Ezra. Something is a little fishy here. Why haven't we ever heard of this before? You're describing one of the most momentous events that could ever happen, claiming that it happened to our ancestors – and we never heard about it?"

"Sure. It was along time ago. Of course you never heard about it."

"C'mon Ezra! It's impossible that our grandparents or great-grandparents would not have passed down the most significant event in our nation's history to some of the people! How could it be that no one has heard about this up until now?! You're claiming all my ancestors, the entire nation, 3 million people heard God speak and received a set of instructions called the Torah, and none of us have heard about it?! You must be lying."

If one cannot pull off a hoax with regard to a continent sinking, so too one cannot pull off a hoax to convince an entire people that their ancestors experienced the most unique event in all of human history. Everyone would know it's a lie. For thousands of years, Sinai was accepted as central to Jewish history. How else can this be explained? Given that people will not fall for a hoax they know is a lie, how could national revelation have been not only accepted — but faithfully followed with great sacrifice by the vast majority of Jews? The only way a people would accept such a claim is if it really happened. If Sinai did not happen, everyone would know it's a lie and it would never have been accepted. The only way one can ever claim a nation experienced revelation and have it accepted is if it is true.[50]

It is quite apparent from the preceding passage that the revelation at Sinai was a real, historical event. With that being said, it changes the entire paradigm of how we view the world. While other religions depend on an individual or a small group to provide testimony, Judaism has the only instance in history when G-d spoke to a nation.

If one were to argue conversely and say that the Sinai Revelation did not occur, they would then have to argue that the

Jews made up their religion. One would expect that a made-up religion would share traits with religions in the area, and would conform to certain norms. As Rabbi Dovid Gottlieb explains, the Jewish faith in virtually no ways resembles faiths of both the surrounding nations, and other world beliefs at the time. He writes:

Ancient Jewish history comprises at the very least 1000 years from the time of king David to the destruction of the second Temple. For approximately ninety percent of this period, i.e. for all but the exile in Babylon, there was a large concentration of Jewish population and an independent Jewish state in the land of Israel. What is striking about this period is the unparalleled uniqueness of Jewish belief. Principles shared by virtually every ancient culture contrast sharply with Jewish sources. The general agreement among other cultures is due to two factors. First, their beliefs reflect common circumstances (the constants in the human condition in the ancient world – birth, death, war and peace, dependence upon poorly understood natural phenomena, etc.). Second, cultures in contact affect one another: ideas are borrowed and mutually modified. Judaism is assumed to have shared the first factor with all other cultures, and its geographical position ("the crossroads of three continents") made it extraordinarily susceptible to the second. Its uniqueness is thus very difficult to explain. What follows are six examples of distinctive Jewish beliefs.

1. Monotheism. Polytheistic idolatry is the rule in ancient religions. The restriction of worship to a single deity is almost unknown . The reason is simple: natural phenomena are so disparate that they are inevitably assigned to different deities, and then each of those deities must be served or else the natural forces under their control will injure the errant community. The uncompromising commitment of Judaism to one G-d only is without parallel in the ancient world.

2. Exclusivity. Each ancient nation had its own pantheon of gods. But each recognized the appropriateness of other nations worshipping its own pantheon. The universalism, and consequent exclusivity of Judaism are absent from ancient religions. Thus, aside from Antiochus' attempt to eliminate Judaism, there are no religious wars in the ancient world! When one country conquered another the second was usually required to acknowledge the chief god of the conqueror, and the conquered were usually happy to comply: the very fact that they lost the war proved that the others' chief god was very powerful. The rest of the religion of the conquered nation was left intact. Only the Jews proclaimed a universal and exclusive concept of deity: our G-d is the only one, all others are fantasy.

3. Spirituality. Ancient religions associated gods very closely with physical objects and/or phenomena. They abound in nature deities: gods of the sun, moon, sea, fertility, death etc. Often the gods are given human form. The only ancient religion to declare that G-d has no physical embodiment, form or likeness is Judaism.

4. G-d as absolute. Ancient religions picture the gods as limited in power. Many start with a genealogy of the gods. That means that certain powers predate them and are out of their control. Only Judaism understands G-d as the creator of all that exists and completely unlimited in His power over creation.

5. Morality. The gods of the ancient world are pictured as petty tyrants acting out their all-too-human desires in conflict with men and with one another. No condition of absolute moral perfection applies to those gods. Only the Jewish G-d is defined as meeting that description.

6. Anti-homosexuality. All ancient cultures permitted some forms of homosexuality, and for many it had religious application. The only exception is Judaism which opposed all forms of homosexuality, whether religious or merely hedonistic.

To ancient cultures, these Jewish beliefs appeared absurd. They contradicted the common experience and convictions of all mankind. Maintaining them branded Jews as quixotic outcasts. The historical problem is to explain how a people originated and preserved so extreme a set of beliefs without being overwhelmed by the unanimous consensus of all other nations.

This problem cannot be solved by appeal to the general success of Jewish cultural achievement. The Jewish nation did not enjoy any outstanding secular success which could have served as the means of preserving Judaism. There was no far-flung Jewish empire, no revolutionary innovations in mathematics, medicine, economics, architecture, the arts, philosophy etc. Had there been such, we might have explained the survival of Judaism as a mere accompaniment of an otherwise successful society.[51]

This provides further evidence that something outside the norm had to establish the Jewish religion. It varies enormously with the religions of the surrounding countries, and inspired such disdain for idolatry to lead the nation to war numerous times. What event could inspire such unique passions? I think the evidence shows clearly that the Sinai Revelation is responsible.

Part B: Fulfilled Prophecies regarding the Jewish national course of events

Prophecy is perhaps the most effective means by which one can see that there is more at play here than meets the materialist eye. The fundamental question that must be asked when evaluating prophecies or predictions is "Would this have been likely to occur without supernatural intervention?" Keeping this question in mind, we must address the specifics offered by Jewish Text. The Torah, the sacred books of Judaism, predicted in highly accurate and specific terms all that has happened in Jewish history. While there are enough accurate predictions to fill volumes, I will address a select few so that I may whet your thirst for evidence.

The Torah clearly and accurately predicts what would happen to the Jewish People if they turned away from their covenant with G-d: Exile and dispersion. The Ramban provides this commentary on Devarim 28:4 [Torah text underlined]:

"The Lord will bring upon you a nation from afar, from the end of the earth, who will swoop down like an eagle": This alludes to the coming of the Romans, who came
from very far [not to mention that the Roman military insignia was an Eagle].[52]

The Torah continues:

"And G-d shall scatter you among all peoples, from one end of the earth to the other"[53]

It is quite easy to see that this prophecy was fulfilled, as the Jews turned away from G-d. Then Rome sacked Jerusalem, with the symbol of the eagle predicted in the preceding verse forming the insignia for their army, and (in an unprecedented manner) caused the dispersal of the Jewish people to every country. For any other people, such widespread diaspora would lead to total assimilation within a few generations (If you need proof of that, ask yourself why there are no ethnic Babylonians today). For the Jewish people, though, diaspora was the beginning, not the end. The Torah predicts this remarkable survival entirely, as it states:

Yet, even then, when they are in the land of their enemies, I will not reject them or spurn them so as to destroy them, annulling My covenant with them:for I the Lord am their G-d[54]

Despite all common sense dictating to the contrary, Jews have managed to maintain strong bonds as a nation, even with thousands of years without shared surroundings, without shared language, and without shared culture, all of which form the backbone of what a nation is. Throughout all of history, dispersion into another's land meant the end of yourself as a separate and culturally distinct people. It is simply too difficult to maintain one's own culture when uprooted from your homes and forced into a new lifestyle. The Jews though, were promised by G-d to remain a separate nationhood, which has been fulfilled even unto today. The Jewish people have endured where all others have failed, in surviving while maintaining one's own culture. It is important to note that another prophecy has therein been fulfilled; the prediction that the Jewish People would remain a small nation but survive nonetheless. Referencing the (then future, now past) exiles of the Jews, the Torah explains:

You shall be left a scant few, after having been as numerous as the stars in the skies, because you did not heed the command of the Lord your G-d[55]

This tale of survival can either be a stroke of incredible luck, both for the Jewish people and for the "writer" of the Torah, or it can be interpreted as divine providence in human affairs. Perhaps even more astounding is the fact that the modern establishment of the Jewish State of Israel was predicted by the Torah as the means by which the Jews would return to their land. This is, from a secular viewpoint, pure nonsense. I'm sure you would agree, that the chances of a tiny and fractured coming together from around the world and forming one of the most advanced countries Earth has ever seen is miniscule. And yet, the Torah predicted it. The Torah says:

[G-d] will bring you together again from all the peoples where the Lord your G-d has scattered you. Even if your outcasts are at the ends of the world, from there the Lord your G-d will gather you, from there He will fetch you. And the Lord your G-d will bring you to the land that your fathers possessed, and you shall possess it; and He will make you more prosperous and more numerous than your fathers.[56]

So what we have determined so far is that the Jewish People were exiled, in perfect alignment with the Torah predictions, survived the exile against overwhelming odds, and returned to their land over 1,800 years later. Looking back at the question posed at the beginning of this section, we must answer whether this course of events was likely without divine intervention. In my view, there are a number of reasons to think that Jewish history has divine support:

First, Multiple Exiles

The Jewish People were exiled from the Land of Israel twice; once in 586 BCE by the Babylonians, and having subsequently returned from the first exile, were exiled again in 70 AD by the Romans, as noted above. These events are interesting for several reasons. First, The Jews are the only people in the history of the world that have been expelled from their land twice in a totalistic fashion.

While other nations were conquered and taxed, the Jews were conquered and driven out from the land. This falls perfectly in-line with the aforementioned Torah prediction, but fails to pass common sense; why would the Romans effectively eliminate a tax base of millions of people? It defies reason, and it is plain to see that there is something going on behind the scenes.

Second, Surviving Exile

Now we have already established the immense unlikelihood a nation would survive one, let alone two exiles. There is not a single example in the world of such a feat being done, and this fact is made all the more astounding when realizing that the Second Jewish Exile lasted from the year 70 AD, all the way to 1948, with the establishment of Modern Israel. The exile lasted 1,878 years. It is such a long period of time that it is difficult to put it into context, but lets see if we can elucidate the significance. Let's take the Irish immigration into the US in the early 1900s as an example. They faced enormous discrimination, were denied employment, and were culturally different than those around them. What was the result? Certainly, it wasn't that the Irish cloistered themselves away from society, as that would have most likely lead to even more negative backlash. The Irish did what every nation finding themselves in a new land has done throughout history, except for the Jews: Assimilate. The Irish became American like the rest of us, and within a generation or two most of the stigma was gone. This is just over a period of 50 to 75 years. The remarkable thing about the Jews, is that they survived an exile that was unimaginably longer, with religious identity and beliefs intact. This is such an enormous feat that its very occurrence alone constitutes a miracle. Rabbenu Bachya explains:

If somebody nowadays were to seek something comparable to the revelation of Godly mercies in the Exodus from Egypt, he should critically study the phenomenon of our survival among the nations. For we deny all their beliefs, both publicly and covertly, as they well know. He would then see that, so far as our daily bread is concerned, our standard of living is similar to theirs. It is just as God promised us: "And yet for all that, when they are in the land of their enemies, I will not reject them, neither will I abhor them, to destroy them utterly..." (Vayikra 26:44). Or as Ezra put it, "For we are slaves, yet in our bondage God has not forsaken us" (Ezra 9:9).[57]

As you can see in the trend, the Torah predicted the survival of Torah through the exiles. The Prophet Isaiah writes:

And this shall be My covenant with them, said the LORD: My spirit which is upon you, and the words which I have placed in your mouth, shall not be absent from your mouth, nor from the mouth of your children, nor from the mouth of your children's children-- said the LORD-- from now on, for all time [58]

Jewish survival and preservation throughout the exiles is nothing short of a miracle; despite the pressures of assimilation, the swords and guns of brutish men, and economic hardship, the Jewish people lived and continued on, just as the Torah indicated it would.

Third, Returning to The Land of Israel

It reads like something out of a novel; the downtrodden and weary nation returns to its ancestral home, fights for independence, and wins decisively. The fledgling state becomes a technological and military powerhouse, and is the sole beacon of freedom and justice in the region. Well, that is exactly what happened to the Jewish People. Nearly 2,000 years of waiting paid off, and the Jewish People returned home, as predicted. But there was immediate danger: all of the surrounding Arab states invade with militaries that are better equipped, better trained, and far superior in numbers. Somehow, Israel not only wins, but conquers large territories from the aggressing Arab countries. The same scenario occurs in 1967, when Israel defeats its Arab neighbors in a ridiculously fast time of 6 days. In 1973, Israel got surprised by invasion forces, on the holiest day of the Jewish calendar, but nonetheless emerged victorious. The simple fact is, Israel has returned to the Land of Israel, and it isn't going anywhere. Certainly, there are indications of divine intervention on behalf of the state. As the Prophet Amos wrote:

I will restore My people Israel. They shall rebuild ruined cities and inhabit them; They shall plant vineyards and drink their wine; They shall till gardens and eat their fruits. And I will plant them upon their soil

Nevermore to be uprooted From the soil I have given them, said the L-RD your G-d[59]

Looking at a big picture analysis, I find that it is quite clear that it is more likely than not that G-d is intervening on behalf of the Jewish people. To clarify this, lets suppose G-d does not exist, and see what realities we are left trying to explain:

1. A book just happened to accurately predict large-scale geopolitical happenings.

2. A small tribe of shepherds from the middle east survived thousands of years of exile despite no other group ever being able to do the same thing.

3. The decedents of the shepherds established a state in the ancestral homeland of their people, despite opposition from neighboring countries and ruling officials.

4. This newborn state, possessing very few weapons and equipment, successfully fought off no less than five better equipped countries that had a sizable man-power advantage.

5. This state continues to win wars frequently against its neighbors, even when surprised, outgunned, and outmanned.

6. This state becomes one of the most advanced in the world in a span of 60 years.

These are just a small sampling of the realities that must be addressed if there is no G-d. But a fair an honest evaluation of the evidence strongly indicates that G-d does indeed exist, and is aiding Israel. There are simply no naturalistic explanations for how well Israel has done, against all odds.

Part C: Archeological Findings

Perhaps most interesting and surprising of all the evidence for the existence of G-d is that historical record presented in the Torah is highly accurate, and has never been shown to be wrong. I will show this through two distinct areas: The general scope of history, and the specifics of the Plagues and the Exodus. The best way in which to test whether the Biblical story is myth is to see if the historicity of the text can be established in relation to other facts we know about the area. If they differ widely, it is likely that the stories are myth and not real historical occurrences. As Rabbi Dovid Gottlieb shows, though, the historicity of the test is superb, and has been *confirmed many times. He writes:*

One of the ways that you can tell if this myth-making goes on is that the people writing the myth project into the past their own conditions of existence. They didn't know that 500-1000 years before life was very different. They assumed that life was more or less the same as their conditions of life and projected backwards. Then, what we find from archaeology is that the conditions were quite different from what was described in the myth, and we know therefore that it was a myth. For example, they may have projected back weapons that they didn't have, domesticated animals that they didn't have, trade routes that they didn't have, settlements that they didn't have and so on. That is how you determine if it was myth. So there was the same assumption about the Biblical account of history before David and Solomon.

But in the case of the Bible, archaeology has revealed the exact opposite. Archaeology has uncovered a myriad of details, details that the Bible records about the quality of life and the conditions of life of the Patriarchs which turn out to be accurate to the last detail. These details are accurate in ways that are utterly inexplicable if you think that this is a normal process of myth formation.

So, for example, Abraham in all his wanderings is never associated with the Northern part of Israel, only the Southern part of Israel. Now in the period to which Abraham is assigned by the Bible, the Northern part of Israel wasn't settled. Later, when supposedly the myth was being made up, it was settled. If someone were writing it later, and projecting his conditions of existence on the past, there would be no reason for him to discriminate against the Northern part of Israel.

Another example: the names Abraham, Isaac, Jacob, Lavan, and Joseph were in common usage in the Patriarchal period and dropped out of usage thereafter. These names appear in archaeological inscriptions from that period and no later period. In the Bible those names are used only in the book of Genesis. Now, somebody five hundred years later is supposed to be making up this myth. How is it that he just happened to get right names for that period of time?

It was custom in that period of time that if a couple was childless, the husband would take a handmaid of the wife as a concubine and have children with her. If the original wife were then to have a child, the child of the handmaid was protected by law against being disinherited. This legal protection did not exist in later centuries. In the Bible, we have Abraham and Sarah doing this. If a handmaid had a child in the manner just described, the law of the time forbade expelling of the child of the handmaid. This explains why, when Sarah told Abraham to throw Ishmael out of the house, the Torah says that it was "Very evil in Abraham's eyes." It was very evil because it went against the local prevailing law. It wasn't forbidden in later centuries, but in that century it was forbidden. If this had been made up five hundred years later and projected onto the past, it would be inexplicable how they could have gotten this right.

An argument that they used that the account depicted in the Bible was a myth was the idea of camels being domesticated. The

Patriarchs are described as having used camels for transportation. It was assumed that this was an anachronism. Camels were domesticated later, but of course the later people didn't know that their ancestors didn't have camels, and if they had camels they would of course have pictured their ancestors as having camels. Their great ancestors couldn't be less than they were.

But, it turns out that this was just archaeological ignorance. We have the eighteenth century B.C.E. Canophorin tablets in Northern Syria which list the domesticated animals and in which the camel is specifically mentioned. Another archaeological discovery depicts a camel in a kneeling position. A seal dating back to this period depicts a rider sitting on a camel. So, it turns out to be an accurate report of the details, not a later anachronistic projection into the past.

There are many examples dealing with Joseph. Take for example the price of a slave. Joseph is sold for twenty pieces of silver. That was the accurate price of a slave in

Joseph's time, and at no other time. Slaves were cheaper beforehand, and they got increasingly more and more expensive later. Imagine someone five hundred years later putting in that detail. How would he know what the price of slaves were five hundred years earlier? He certainly wouldn't get it right by accident.

You have the same thing regarding sleeping in Egypt on beds. In Palestine at that time they slept on the ground, and in Egypt they slept on beds, and so therefore the Torah mentions explicitly that when Jacob was in Egypt, he died on a bed.

The investiture of Joseph as viceroy in Egypt follows the pattern from that period. He stood before Pharaoh and had to be shaved because the Pharaohs in that period were shaved. He had a collar put around his neck and a ring put on his finger. There are hieroglyphs of that specific procedure, and of riding in a chariot second to the king. All of these details are accurate.[60]

With that in mind, we can see that the text clearly passes the bar for correctness in dealing with both the time period and its details. If the text were a myth, it would be highly unlikely for an individual to do the research necessary to make such an accurate text (and arguably, such research would have been impossible in the era it was written). Accordingly, its accuracy becomes strong evidence for belief in G-d, based upon the details of the text. As if this was not enough, we will delve into the specifics of the Ten Plagues and Exodus narrative, and we shall see that not only is the text accurate, but it is supported by other, unrelated depictions of the events. The Ten Plagues and the Exodus form the backbone of the Jewish historical narrative. Evidence to support them should therefore be taken as direct evidence for G-d's involvement in Jewish History, and accordingly as evidence that He exists. Rabbi and International Lecturer Lawrence Kelemen has extensively studied the evidence for the Exodus Miracles and Ten Plagues, using Egyptian and other local records and texts to determine the truth. He writes the following, in his book "Permission to Receive":

Two separate Egyptian papyri testify to the Nile's turning to blood. Egyptologist Dr. James Pritchard published one in 1950, "The Admonitions of an Egyptian Sage," and Egyptologist M. Lichtheim published the other in 1980, "Setne Khamwas and Si-osire." In Exodus 10, God instructs Moses to stretch out his hand toward the heavens and thus stimulate a "plague of darkness." Moses follows God's order, and, the Torah says, "there was a thick darkness in all Egypt" for several days. Dr. Donald Redford, professor of Near Eastern Studies at the University of Toronto, tells us that "sources contemporary with the expulsion... apprise us of curious atmospheric disturbances, strange for the Nile valley." He describes a "snippet of a diary preserved on the verso of the Rhind Mathematical Papyrus [which] records the events leading up to the fall of Avaris," Avaris being the Egyptian capital city close to biblical Goshen.The diary's author complained that "darkness covered the western heavens...and for a period of days no light shone in the two lands." Redford confesses that "the striking resemblance between this catastrophic storm and some of the traditional plagues seems more than fortuitous."

At the 1987 meeting of the Near East Archaeological Society, Dr. Hans Goedicke, professor of Near Eastern Studies at Johns Hopkins University, spoke about an inscription found on an ancient religious shrine at El-Arish, near modem Gaza. The shrine had been brought there from Egypt's Goshen region in 626 B.C.E. as part of frantic efforts to solicit the gods' assistance in fortifying Egypt's eastern border against an impending Persian attack. The inscription reads, 'There was no stepping out into the open for a period of nine days...one face could not see its equal." Pritchard's collection also includes an ancient Egyptian papyrus, "Prophecies of Neferti," describing the same phenomenon.

Dr. John Wilson, professor of Near Eastern Studies at che University of Chicago, translated another papyrus relevant to the plagues, The Admonitions of Ipu-Wer," also published in Pritchard's Ancient Near Eastern Texts. According to its first possessor (Anastasi), it was found in ancient Egyptian Memphis. In 1828 the Museum of Leyden (Netherlands) acquired the document. The papyrus offers a blow-by-blow description of an Egyptian dynasty's wildly destructive end, resembling...the biblical narrative. The text provides a graphic portrait of the Nile flowing with blood: "If one drinks of it [the river of blood], one rejects it as human [blood].

Like the biblical record of fire that descended from heaven during the plague of hail, Ipu-Wer recounts how "doors, columns...are burned up...fire has mounted up on high." Also reminiscent of the biblical hail that "destroyed all the outdoor plants," the Egyptian eyewitness exclaims, "Grain has perished on every side.... Everybody says: 'There is nothing!"

The Torah tells us that when the Israelites finally left Egypt, "They requested silver and gold articles and clothing from the Egyptians...draining Egypt of its wealth." Ipu-Wer complains that:

"The robber is now the possessor of riches.... Gold is lacking.... Behold, the owners of robes are now in rags. But he who never wove for himself is now the owner of fine linen.... Behold, she who had not even a box is now the owner of a trunk."

The Torah also relates that after the seventh plague a few Egyptians, disgruntled over the plagues, protested to Pharaoh to let the Israelites leave. Ipu-Wer moans, "Ah, would that 1 had raised my voice at that time -- it might have saved me from the suffering in which I am!"

Before the final biblical plague, the death of the first-bom, Moses warns Pharaoh, "It will be something that your fathers and your fathers' fathers have never seen since the day they were in the land." Ipu-Wer similarly mourns, "Some¬thing has been done which never happened for a long time...the once prayed-for children are now laid out on the high ground."[61]

There is additional evidence for these occurrences. The Layden Papyrus #334, dating to ancient Egypt and found in the 1800s, tells a striking history remarkably similar to the Torah narrative. It states:

"Plague is throughout the land. Blood is everywhere. The river is blood. Men shrink from tasting it... That is our water, that is our happiness. What should we do in respect thereof? All is ruined...Gates, columns and walls are consumed by fire. Egypt weeps, the entire palace is without revenues...Grain has perished on every side...All animals their hearts weep. Cattle moan, cattle went astray, there's none to gather them together...The land is without light...The children of princes are dashed against the wall. The children of princes are cast out into the streets...He who places his brother in the ground is everywhere. There is

groaning throughout the land mingled with lamentations."[62]

As if this was not evidence enough for the historicity of the exodus, An Ancient Egyptian shrine from el-Arish confirms the final Egyptian stage of the exodus:

Pharaoh is described as marching, together with his army, to the eastern part of the kingdom, where he was engulfed by a whirlpool.[63]

From this, it is clear that there is good historical reason to believe that the plagues occurred. Egyptian sources, who are even more likely to hide such a defeat as the plagues, are recorded lamenting their massive loss. The Torah account is proven to be highly accurate, and thus we may draw upon its knowledge. Accordingly, one may safely agree that the plagues happened, and they were performed by G-d as dictated in the Torah.

Part D: Fulfilled Prophecies regarding World Events and Nature

So far we have addressed prophecies dealing with the actual course of events that the Jewish people experience. In this section, we will address more prophecies that have been fulfilled, ranging in content from animals to history itself. For each prediction, you must ask yourself, "Is it more likely than not someone would be able to guess the prediction?"

Example 1: Fins and Scales

One unique aspect of Judaism as a religion is that it makes claims that are testable; there are certain statements made in the Talmud, the Jewish Oral Law that, should Torah not be divine, should easily be proven wrong. Take the following Talmudic statement for instance:

"[A fish that] has scales has fins, but there are some that have fins and no scales"[64]

This tells us that all fish with scales have fins, and there are no fish that have scales without fins. Now, this should be a trivial task to resolve and quickly disprove an important Jewish text; unfortunately for the critic, the fact of the matter is that it is entirely true. Thousands of years of science, zoology, and biology have yielded much advancement, but the Talmudic decree has yet to be disproven; all fish with scale have fins. It certainly seems reasonable that a fish could have scales with no fins, but there are none. So we are left with the question of why this is the case. Alas, we will probably never know why there are no fish with scales and no fins, but we do gain something from this exchange. The Talmud makes a direct and easily falsifiable statement regarding a matter of science, and has never been disproven. This lends a great deal of support to Talmudic divinity.

Example 2: The Industrial Revolution

The Zohar, an ancient Jewish religious text dating back thousands of years, predicts:

"In the [Jewish] year 600 of the sixth [year 5600 corresponds to 1840 CE], the gates of wisdom above and the wellsprings of wisdom below will be opened, and the world will prepare to enter the seventh [millennium], just as a person prepares himself toward sunset for the Sabbath...."[65]

In this verse, "The gates of wisdom above" refers to spiritual knowledge, and "the wellsprings of wisdom below" refers to secular knowledge. This is very interesting, as 1840 year corresponds to the beginning of the industrial revolution, a time of great discovery and innovation that completely changed the world for the better.

Example 3: False Gods

Oftentimes, the answer is right under your nose, and you can't see the truth. In regards to religion, the Torah tells us specifically to avoid the false prophets and teachings of those that would come later on. First, the Torah does so generically:

If there appears among you a prophet or a dream- diviner and he gives you a sign or a portent, saying, "Let us follow and worship another god"-- whom you have not experienced-- even if the sign or portent that he named to you comes true, do not heed the words of that prophet or that dream- diviner. For the LORD your God is testing you to see whether you really love the LORD your God with all your heart and soul[66].

Seems reasonable enough; G-d commands us to not pay attention to those that would turn us away from the proper path. Where warning becomes prophecy is where it becomes telling. The Torah continues:

The LORD will scatter you among the peoples, and only a scant few of you shall be left among the nations to which the LORD will drive you. There you will serve man-made gods of wood and stone, that cannot see or hear or eat or smell[67]

We are warned that, when the Jews are exiled among the nations, they will try to convert them to worship Gods of wood and stone. Its not hard to see what this means. The world's largest religion, Christianity, worships a God of the (wooden) cross. The adherents of the second largest religion, Islam, bow and pray to a stone in the kaaba in Mecca. In plain english, clear as day, we are warned that Christianity and Islam will try to lead the Jewish people away. Keep in mind the Torah (even according to secular authorities) is aged at hundreds or thousands of years before Christianity and Islam became existent. As such, we have a perfect prediction that not only identifies who we are talking about, but conforms to the scope of history, between crusades and pogroms.

Fourth, The Expanding Universe

Now, it is commonly accepted by virtually everyone that the Universe began with the Big Bang, and that the Earth "sits" in the void of space. This was not always the case, though. Until the mid-20th Century, scientists believed the universe to be eternal, and it was not until overwhelming scientific evidence forced their hand did they recant and accept that the universe had a beginning. Since this beginning, the universe has been stretching and expanding, turning the beginning point of near infinite heat and pressure into everything we see today. Interestingly, the Jews knew this thousands of years ago.

Two examples are: "(G-d) Who stretches out the heavens like a curtain..." (Psalms 104:3), and "And forgettest the L-rd, thy maker, that has stretched forth the heavens... (Isaiah 51:13)." Accordingly, we can see that even in the ancient past, the Jewish people knew that the Universe was being stretched and expanded.

These examples provide even further proof that the Torah is divine, and along with that, that G-d exists. Without G-d existing, one would be forced into terrible leaps of logic to justify how the Jewish people have always seemingly known the unknowable.

Example 5: The Hidden Face of G-d

The greatest root of disbelief in G-d in the modern era, other than a simple desire to avoid accountability to a higher power, is that we do not see miracles today the way that our ancestors described them. While one could argue that the happenings with the State of Israel are indeed a miracle, given her survival and flourishing, there is certainly something left to be desired when we learn stories of G-d splitting the ocean for the Jews to escape Egypt, and instead in the modern era we hear only silence. The naturalistic explanation for this discrepancy between stories of old times, and modern experience, is that in the present we have simply advanced science sufficiently to no longer "need" G-d as an explanation. The problem with this is that science will never have all the answers, and there is little in the way of critical discourse between opposing parties. Even so, science can be a valuable tool to improve our quality of life. That being said, science has not been able to rule out G-d, so the question remains: Why do we not experience G-d directly today? The Torah explains explicitly that G-d's concealment from what we experience is a direct result of the immoral behavior performed by Jews, in forsaking the covenant made with G-d. It reads:

Then My anger will flare up against them, and I will abandon them and hide My countenance from them. They shall be ready prey; and many evils and troubles shall befall them. And they shall say on that day, "Surely it is because our God is not in our midst that these evils have befallen us." Yet I will keep My countenance hidden on that day, because of all the evil they have done in turning to other gods.[68]

With yet another successful prediction, the Torah tells us that over time, Jews will stray from G-d, and that will cause him to conceal himself from us. Lets analyze this prediction. Now, if the Torah was not given by G-d and was instead written by a random person thousands of years ago, one would expect the telling of the future to be much like the present was at the time. The writer wouldn't know that the supernatural would appear to be disproven, and therefore the prediction is surprising. One would not expect someone from a time period of little scientific growth to foresee the future that results from accelerated growth. Accordingly, this prediction serves as a good indication as to why G-d seems to be absent.

Section IV: Responses to Atheistic Arguments

Argument 1: The Problem of Evil and Pain

The Problem of Evil is an argument as old as the belief in G-d itself. There are a number of forms of this argument, but most of them depend on the same premises. First it is fitting to give a general overview of what the argument says. Basically, G-d is supposedly all-powerful and entirely good, and yet our world is full of evil and pain. If G-d existed, he would not allow this, and therefore G-d does not exist. At face value, this argument is very enticing to those struggling with their belief, as it seems to be intuitively true. Upon closer inspection, though, it fails to hold water. The first exposition of the Problem of Evil I will address is the most simple, and was presented J.L. Mackie. He writes:

"In its simplest form the problem is this: God is omnipotent; God is wholly good; and yet evil exists. There seems to be some contradiction between these three

propositions, so that if any two of them were true the third would be false."[69]

This argument is really just an appeal to contradictions which do not in fact exist. Examining closely, we can see that all three premises are indeed true; G-d is omnipotent, G-d is entirely good, and evil does exist. Mackie claims that these three ideas cannot all be true, but that is most certainly not the case. Professor William Lane Craig elaborates:

According to the logical problem of evil, it is logically impossible for God and evil to co-exist. If God exists, then evil cannot exist. If evil exists, then God cannot exist. Since evil exists, it follows that God does not exist. But the problem with this argument is that there's no reason to think that God and evil are logically incompatible. There's no explicit contradiction between them. But if the atheist means there's some implicit contradiction between God and evil, then he must be assuming some hidden premises which bring out this implicit contradiction. But the problem is that no philosopher has ever been able to identify such premises. Therefore, the logical problem of evil fails to prove any inconsistency between God and evil. But more than that: we can actually prove that God and evil are logically consistent. You see, the atheist presupposes that God cannot have morally sufficient reasons for permitting the evil in the world. But this assumption is not necessarily true. So long as it is even possible that God has morally sufficient reasons for permitting evil, it follows that God and evil are logically consistent. And, certainly, this does seem at least logically possible. Therefore, I'm very pleased to be able to report that it is widely agreed among contemporary philosophers that the logical problem of evil has been dissolved. The co-existence of God and evil is logically possible.[70]

Evil is not some mythical creature that precludes the existence of G-d, but is rather a creation of G-d in its own right.

The Jewish Prophet Isaiah confirms this, when he writes:

"I form the light, and create Darkness; I make peace, and create evil; I am the L-rd, That Doeth all These Things."[71]

Accordingly, the proper religious belief in G-d does not mean that evil should not exist, because G-d himself made evil. But of course, that will not satisfy the atheist, because the veracity of the Prophets depend on G-d in fact existing. The real question meant by Mackie's formulation of the argument is "Why does G-d allow evil?". This question can be answered with three unique reasons:

First, G-d created humanity so that we would have free will. His intention, as relayed through Torah, Talmud, and other Jewish texts, was to allow us to choose to follow his path of righteousness when presented with the possibility for evil. Given that we do have free will, some of us will indeed choose evil, unfortunately. This is not G-d's fault, as the very fact of creating a being with free will means that undesired consequences may occur. One should therefore not blame G-d for evil, given that evil is perpetuated by man. If G-d were to intercede when evil occurs, we would lose our free will, as we would not have the ability to choose. Too frequently do people blame G-d for bad things that happen, rather than the people doing the actions themselves. Professor Alvin Plantinga of the University of Notre Dame writes:

"A world containing creatures who are significantly free...is more valuable, all else being equal, than a world containing no free creatures at all. Now God can create free creatures, but he can't cause or determine them to do only what is right. For if He does so, then they aren't significantly free after all; they do not do what is right freely. To create creatures capable of moral good, therefore, He must create creatures capable of moral evil; and He can't

give these creatures the freedom to perform evil and at the same time prevent them from doing so...The fact that free creatures sometimes go wrong, however, counts neither against God's omnipotence nor against His goodness; for He could have forestalled the occurrence of moral evil only by removing the possibility of moral good...The heart of the Free Will Defense is the claim that it is possible that God could not have created a universe containing moral good...without creating one that also contained moral evil. And if so, then it is possible that God has good reason for creating a world containing evil."[72]

Second, Evil is a necessary converse of good. If there were no evil, it would be impossible to say something or an action is morally good, as there is nothing to compare it to. To use an analogy, if humans did not need sleep, it would be meaningless to say that "I am awake", as that is the only thing to be. Therefore evil is allowed in the world so that the actions of the righteous are able to be seen as being as great as they truly are.

Third, the evil inclination (or our desire to do evil things that is normally kept in check by our inclination to do good) is necessary for us to strive in life. Our pride and desire for self-preservation requires that we make something of ourselves in the world, and that encourages the advancement of society. Our sexual desires encourage us to seek a mate and start a family, perpetuating the human race. Virtually every desire for evil we have can be linked strongly back to the general idea that if the desire is enacted in a positive manner, it serves to benefit society and humanity as a whole.

In response to these responses to the Mackie Problem of Evil, one might pose the objections that there is evil not caused by free will, or that there is more evil than necessary in the world. I will address each of these individually.

First, Evils not caused by free will are natural evils, such as disease or natural disasters. At a prima facie level, one could argue that these are not truly evils, but rather misfortunes. Even if this is the case, it could be argued by the atheist that these misfortunes should not occur. Either way, the response to this is that natural evils are a necessary component of an imperfect world. If G-d had intended our world to be perfect, we would have nothing to strive for, and would see no need to turn to G-d for support. G-d's intention in creating man must be seen as a way to maximize total good. It is better for a man to choose the right path given the option not to, then to be forced onto that path from the beginning. This is seen in common experience, as we view it as better, for example, if someone chooses a career that they love as opposed to being forced into a job they do not want. If this world was perfect, there would be little incentive for man to seek godliness, as we would have all we need. Instead, we have been given a world that is not easy to survive in, and yet we have not only flourished, but have by and large maintained faith throughout it.

Second, the problem with the assertion that there is more evil than necessary in the world is, that being human, the person making that claim cannot know what the necessary amount of evil is for G-d's plan to have a redemption of humanity, and they are simply asserting such as an emotional appeal. No one knows what the threshold is for evil in the world. It is very possible, and indeed likely, that the amount of evil in the world is precisely what it needs to be to encourage humanity to further relationships with G-d. Another major problem with this assertion is that it ignores the biblically supported idea that G-d allows evil as punishment for Adam and Eve's eating of the forbidden fruit. Even if this would not account for all of the "surplus" evil, certainly there are bad deeds being done today that are worthy of punishment. This aside, if G-d does exist, and there is evil in this world, it is entirely possible that in the afterlife there will be judgment for wrongdoings and rewards for righteousness. There is no reason to exclude this possibility, which virtually all religions agree upon.

In fact, upon hearing of similar responses to his formulation of the Problem of Evil, Mackie wrote:

Since this defense is formally [that is, logically] possible, and its principle involves no real abandonment of our ordinary view of the opposition between good and evil, we can concede that the problem of evil does not, after all, show that the central doctrines of theism are logically inconsistent with one another. [73]

While there are other formulations of this argument, virtually all (if not all) of them can be refuted with the same lines of argumentation. Evil is something that occurs either as a result of free will, or as a natural evil. Free will requires that evil be possible, and thus occurs, and natural evils may be easily explained by the necessity of an imperfect world, uncertainty as to what the "minimum" level of evil must be, the possibility of divine judgment, and divine reward.

The Evil G-d Challenge

The Evil G-d Challenge, presented by Stephen Law, is both easy to understand and easy to refute. In essence, he argues that there could be an infinitely powerful, infinitely knowing being, much like the traditional G-d, but that is perfectly evil instead of perfectly good. He uses this possibility as a means to discredit responses to the Problem of Evil, in stating that if the existence of Evil doesn't disprove an infinitely good G-d, the existence of Good does not rule out the possibility of the existence of an infinitely Evil being. The response to this is quite simple. It is certainly possible that there is an infinitely evil being, that is all powerful and created the universe. But it is less probable then the existence of an infinitely good being, i.e. G-d. This is because we have an overwhelming amount of evidence that indicates that if a G-d exists, he is good. We have the national revelation to the Jewish people, prophecies that have come true, and the very fact that most of life tends to be if not enjoyable, not painful. It would seem likely that if an infinite evil being existed, he would not reveal himself to the people as their protector, and then faithfully serve that role and ensure all promises were fulfilled after thousands of years. Simple put, there is no good reason to believe in an evil creator, while there is good reason to believe in a good one.

Argument 2: The God Delusion Argument/ Who Designed the Designer?

In his book, "The God Delusion", atheist Richard Dawkins presents an attempted syllogism that seeks to be a logically valid argument for the non-existence of G-d. In this section, I will refute the argument thoroughly, focusing on the major flaws he has made. Dawkins argument is as follows:

1. One of the greatest challenges to the human intellect has been to explain how the complex, improbable appearance of design in the universe arises.

2. The natural temptation is to attribute the appearance of design to actual design itself.

3. The temptation is a false one because the designer hypothesis immediately raises the larger problem of who designed the designer.

4. The most ingenious and powerful explanation is Darwinian evolution by natural selection.

5. We don't have an equivalent explanation for physics.

6. We should not give up the hope of a better explanation arising in physics, something as powerful as Darwinism is for biology.

Therefore, God almost certainly does not exist.[74]

The first premise I take issue with is the third; Dawkins entirely dismissed G-d based on the poorly formed question "Who Made G-d?". With trivial amounts of thinking, this argument can be entirely refuted. The Torah tells us, in the very first verse, than G-d created the heavens and the Earth, "in the beginning". The beginning of what? Well, the only answer that makes sense is that it is the absolute beginning: the beginning of time. Therefore, G-d existed before time, in the Judaic tradition. If G-d exists before time, he certainly would not be bound by the time-based laws of cause and effect! G-d has always existed, because for him, there is no reason for him to have started to exist: he has always been, since the beginning. Modern science supports the idea that time had a beginning with the Big Bang. Accordingly, Dawkins' argument fails entirely, because asking who designed the designer is like asking "What was your favorite color before you were conceived?"

Namely, it fails to follow logically. The next area to address is premises 5, 6, and the conclusion. Now it should be very apparent to the reader that the conclusion does not follow from the premises. The possibility a theory of physics which is revolutionary will be made does not in any way refute G-d. Indeed, the fact that such a theory has not arisen in Physics is evidence for G-d, as He is the best explanation we have for the origin of the Universe. Even if such a Physics theory were to come in to being, it would not disprove G-d, as science will never be able to answer why the Big Bang occurred, only that it did indeed happen.

Argument 3: God of the Gaps

The "God of the Gaps" argument is common among those that lack belief in G-d. In essence, it says that G-d is only used to explain what isn't yet understood by science, and thus we should reject belief in G-d as an unscientific belief. There are a number of reasons that the God of the Gaps argument is incorrect:

First, Even if it were true that G-d is only used to explain what science cannot, that in no way disproves that G-d exists. It only serves to be a distractor from the real issue at hand, and accordingly should be disregarded. G-d's existence or non-existence cannot be established from an argument that simply says to reject belief; it must provide positive reasons for belief or disbelief. Second, G-d isn't an unscientific hypothesis. While modern atheistic science has transformed from a study of how the world works to a concerted effort to discourage belief in G-d, traditional scientific values, like discovering the truth and tackling the unknown, are very much so compatible with belief in G-d. If the intent is to actually find the truth of our existence, G-d serves as an important means by which we can comprehend the incomprehensible.

Argument 4: The Paradox of Omnipotence

The atheists have long attempted to "disprove" G-d by claiming the existence of certain paradoxes in regard to G-d's existence. These paradoxes generally follow along the logical path of "Could G-d create a rock so heavy he couldn't lift it?" This argument is very simple to refute, and it quickly becomes clear that is hardly suffices as even being an argument at all. The response, in its most basic exposition, is that G-d cannot do the logically impossible, and therefore the paradox does not make any sense in regards to G-d. Now some people may argue that by G-d not being able to contradict logic, that means he is not all-powerful. Again, this is false. G-d is all powerful in that he can do all <u>doable</u> things. This is necessarily G-d's ability because otherwise the discussion rapidly turns nonsensical. For example, someone can't touch a September; the action "touch" simply doesn't apply to "September", which being a month has no physicality to touch. It doesn't make an individual any less able to do things that they can't touch September, and in the same way G-d is still all-powerful, despite not being able to make a round square or a married bachelor. These things simply cannot exist by their very nature. Rabbi Saadia Gaon furthers on the idea that G-d can do all that is logically possible, as he writes:

His praises and His glorifications are only with understandable and upright things, not with exaggeration and absurdity such as "He who can make five more than ten without adding to it", or "He who can fit the entire world into the hole of a ring without shrinking the former or enlarging the latter", or "He who can make the past into the future", for all these things are absurdities. Perhaps several heretics will ask us about this. We will respond to them "He has the ability to do all things, but that which you mentioned - that is not a thing; it is an absurdity, and an absurdity is not anything."[75]

The Paradox of Omnipotence is an argument that to anyone with a cursory understanding of G-d can refute, but it is still a very popular argument because people are afraid of saying G-d is "unable" to do something. The reality is that G-d is unlimited in any logically coherent way.

Conclusion

At the beginning of this paper, I asked you to evaluate its arguments through a mindset of "What is more likely, G-d's existence or non-existence?". As I have demonstrated, there is overwhelming evidence of all types to suggest G-d exists. The design and very existence of the Universe, the development of human life, consciousness, and NDEs, as well as massive historical evidence for the Torah. To deny that G-d exists consistently, you would have to justify why it is more likely that seemingly impossibly occurrence happen, than the simpler and more complete explanation that G-d exists. It is undoubtably difficult to accept that G-d exists when you have had your heart hardened by functional eons of disbelief, but in light of the significant evidence presented, I implore you to open your mind.

Endnotes

---

1. Summa Theologica, First Part, Second Question, Third Article
2. Dr. Dennis Scania, Cambridge University Observatories, BBC's "The Anthropic Principle"

3. Robin Collins, "A Scientific Argument for the Existence of God: The Fine-Tuning Design Argument," in Michael J. Murray, editor, Reason for the Hope Within (Grand Rapids, Mich.: Eerdmans, 1999), 48.

4. Roger Penrose, the Rouse Ball Professor of Mathematics at the University of Oxford, http://www.geraldschroeder.com/FineTuning.aspx

5. Hugh Ross, "Fine-Tuning for Life in the Universe," Appendix C, Lights in the Sky and Little Green Men (Colorado Springs, CO: NavPress, 2002), in press

6. Strobel, Lee (2009-05-18). The Case for a Creator: A Journalist Investigates Scientific Evidence That Points Toward God (Strobel, Lee) (Kindle Locations 5092-5099). Zondervan. Kindle Edition.

7. Strobel, Lee (2009-05-18). The Case for a Creator: A Journalist Investigates Scientific Evidence That Points Toward God (Strobel, Lee) (Kindle Locations 2373-2392). Zondervan. Kindle Edition.

8. John Leslie, Universes (London: Routledge, 1989), pg. 5
9. Davies, Paul. The Accidental Universe. Cambridge: Cambridge University Press, 1982. Pg 90-91

10. Davis, John Jefferson. "The Design Argument, Cosmic "Fine-tuning," and the Anthropic Principle." The International Journal of Philosophy of Religion. pg. 140

11. Leslie, John. "How to Draw Conclusions From a Fine-Tuned Cosmos." In Robert Russell, et. al., eds., Physics, Philosophy and Theology: A Common Quest for Understanding. Vatican City State: Vatican Observatory Press, pp. 297-312

12. Robin Collins, The Blackwell Companion to Natural Theology, pg. 211-213

13. William Dembski, "The Design Inference", (New York:Cambridge, 1998), pg. 203-214
14. Professor David Plaisted, University of North Carolina, "The Improbability of Abiogenesis", http://www.cs.unc.edu/~plaisted/ce/abiogenesis.html

15. Coppedge, James, F. 1973. Evolution: Possible or impossible? Zondervan, Grand Rapids, MI
16. Francis Crick, University College London, Evolution from Space, p.24

17. I. Prigogine, N. Gregair, A. Babbyabtz, Physics Today 25, pp. 23-28

---

18. Dose, K. (1988) "The Origin of Life: More Questions than Answers," Interdisciplinary Science Reviews, 13, 348.

19. Darwin, C. (1872) Origin of Species, 6th ed. (1988), New York University Press, New York, p. 154.

20. Bruce Alberts, "The Cell as a Collection of Protein Machines," Cell 92 (February 8, 1998).

21. Michael J. Katz, "Templets and the explanation of complex patterns" (Cambridge: Cambridge University Press, 1986)

22. Rana, Fazal (2008-06-01). Cell's Design, The (Reasons to Believe): How Chemistry Reveals the Creator's Artistry (Kindle Locations 1580-1587). Baker Publishing Group. Kindle Edition.

23. Rana, Fazal (2008-06-01). Cell's Design, The (Reasons to Believe): How Chemistry Reveals the Creator's Artistry (Kindle Locations 1500-1502). Baker Publishing Group. Kindle Edition.

24. Rana, Fazal (2008-06-01). Cell's Design, The (Reasons to Believe): How Chemistry Reveals the Creator's Artistry (Kindle Locations 1480-1493). Baker Publishing Group. Kindle Edition

25. Hubert P. Yockey, Information Theory and Molecular Biology (Cambridge: Cambridge University Press, 1992), 180– 83., quoted by Fazal Rana in "Cell's Design",
26. Erwin, D..H., and Valentine, J.W. "'Hopeful

monsters,' transposons, and the Metazoan radiation", Proc. Natl. Acad. Sci USA 81:5482-5483, Sept 1984

27. Detlef D. Leipe, L. Aravind, and Eugene V. Koonin, "Did DNA Replication Evolve Twice Independently?" Nucleic Acids Research 27 (September 1, 1999): 3389– 3401., quoted by Fazal Rana in "Cell's Design",

28. Strobel, Lee (2009-05-18). The Case for a Creator: A Journalist Investigates Scientific Evidence That Points Toward God (Strobel, Lee) (Kindle Locations 5122-5132). Zondervan. Kindle Edition.

29. What Darwin Didn't Know, by Geoffrey Simmons (Harvest House, 2004), 167-176

30. S. Kalir et al., "Ordering Genes in a Flagella Pathway by Analysis of Expression Kinetics from Living Bacteria," Science 292 (June 15, 2001): 2080– 83; Gavin S. Chilcott and Kelly T. Hughes, "Coupling of Flagellar Gene Expression to Flagellar Assembly in Salmonella enterica Serovar Typhimurium and Escherichia coli," Microbiology and Molecular Biology Reviews 64 (December 2000): 694– 708.

31. Behe, Michael J. (2001-04-04). Darwin's Black Box: The Biochemical Challenge to Evolution (Kindle Locations 1092-1103). Free Press. Kindle Edition.

32. K. T. Maslin, An Introduction to the Philosophy

---

of Mind. (Malden, MA: Polity Press, 2001), 180.

33. Moreland and Craig, Philosophical Foundations, 233.

34. Leibniz, G. (1979) Monadology 17. In P. P. Weiner (ed.), Leibniz Selections, 533–551. New York:
Charles Scribner's Sons.

35. J. P. MORELAND, Blackwell Companion to Natural Theology, pg. 240

36. Skinner, B. F. (1990) Can psychology be a science of mind? American Psychologist 45, 1206–10.

37. Kim, J. (1998) Mind in a Physical World. An Essay on the Mind-Body Problem and Mental Causation.
Cambridge, MA: MIT Press. Pg. 98

38. Feser E. (2005) Philosophy of Mind: A Short Introduction. Oxford: Oneworld Press. Pg. 136

39. Ibid, pg.149

40. Lewis, C. S. (1978) Miracles: A Preliminary Study, rev edn. New York: Macmillan. Pg. 19

41. J.B.S. Haldane, Possible Worlds, p. 209

42. "Adventures in Immortality," George Gallup, Jr. and William Proctor, http://curiosity.discovery.com/question/how-common-near-death-experiences

---

43. Patrick Wells, 2011, Quoting: Kenneth Ring, University of Connecticut, "Mindsight",http://www.near-death.com/experiences/experts04.html

44. Dr. Peter Fenwick,"Into the Unknown: Strange but true" http://www.near-death.com/experiences/evidence01.html

45. **"Near-death experience in survivors of cardiac arrest: a prospective study in the Netherlands",** Pim van Lommel et al., http://profezie3m.altervista.org/archivio/TheLancet_NDE.htm

46. Richard Taylor, Ethics, Faith, and Reason (Englewood Cliffs, N.J.: Prentice-Hall, 1985), pg. 83-84.

47. (Deut. 4:32-36)

48. (Deut. 4:32-33)

49. Rabbi Nechemia Coopersmith and Rabbi Moshe Zeldman, "Did G-d Speak at Sinai?", Aish, http://www.aish.com/jl/p/ph/Did_God_Speak_at_Sinai.html

50. Ibid.

51. Rabbi Dovid Gottlieb, Living Up to the Truth, Ch. 7: "Jewish Survival - The Fact and its implications", http://ohr.edu/2055

52. Ramban's Torah Commentary, Devarim 28:4

53. Devarim 28:64

54. Vayikra 26:44

55. Devarim 28:62

56. Devarim 30:1-5

57. Rabbenu Bachya, Sha'ar Ha-Bechinah, Chapter 5

58. Isaiah 59:21

59. Amos 9:14-15

60. Rabbi Dovid Gottlieb, "Living up to the Truth", Chaper 5: Archeology, http://www.ohr.edu/2053

61. Lawrence Kelemen, "Permission to Receive", 1996, pg. 103-106.

62. The Layden Papyrus #334

63. The Final Resolution, by Gershon Alswang, pgs 14-20

64. Talmud, Niddah 51b

65. I Zohar 117a

66. Devarim 13:2-4

67. Devarim 4:27-28

68. Devarim 31:17-18

www.ingramcontent.com/pod-product-compliance
Lightning Source LLC
Chambersburg PA
CBHW060923040426
42445CB00011B/764

* 9 7 8 0 6 1 5 9 0 9 3 1 8 *

69. Mackie, J.L. 1955. "Evil and Omnipotence, Mind 64: 200-212

70. William Lane Craig, "The Problem of Evil", http://www.reasonablefaith.org/the-problem-of-evil#ixzz2i6ymC9lw

71. Isaiah 45:7

72. Alvin Plantinga,"Free Will Defense", Philosophy in America. Ithaca: Cornell UP / London: Allen & Unwin, 196

73. Mackie, J. L. 1982. The Miracle of Theism. Oxford: Oxford University Press.

74. Richard Dawkins, "The God Delusion", pg. 157-158

75. Rabbi Saadia Gaon, "Emunoth ve-Deoth", Ch. 2